FIASCO AT FREDERICKSBURG

FIASCO AT
FREDERICKSBURG

VORIN E. WHAN, JR.

Reprinted with permission by
The Pennsylvania State University

Olde Soldier Books, Inc.
I8779 North Frederick Road
Gaithersburg, Md. 20879

ISBN 1-56013-013X

TO LYN

CONTENTS

Introduction   xi

   I. The Armies   1

  II. The Antagonists   4

 III. Antietam and After   15

 IV. Calm Before the Storm   29

  V. Valor on the Bridges   37

 VI. The Battlefield   47

VII. Blueprint for Victory—or Disaster   51

VIII. Franklin Begins the Assault   59

 IX. Sumner and the Stone Wall   77

  X. Saving the Army   102

Appendices

  A. Organization of the Armies   115

  B. Recapitulation of Losses   121

  C. Tactical Study   124

Bibliography   139

Notes   149

MAPS

1. Virginia Theater of Operations   14

2. Valley of the Rappahannock   17

3. Bridge Sites and Covering Artillery Batteries   28

4. Fredericksburg Battle Area   48

5. Burnside's Plan of Battle   52

6. Prospect Hill and Vicinity   60

7. Fredericksburg and Vicinity   76

8. Stone Wall and Vicinity   78

The photograph on the end papers is a view of
the battlefield looking northeast from the southern end of Willis Hill.

INTRODUCTION

In reading this book, one might well keep in mind the Japanese proverb, "Woe unto him who has not tasted defeat," for in victory the mistakes made are often unappreciated and forgotten. Only by a study of the causes of our defeats can the lessons learned at so great cost be fully utilized.

In the four-year struggle to preserve the Union, the United States Army suffered one of its most disheartening defeats in the Battle of Fredericksburg, December 11-16, 1862. Although the Unionists made many mistakes in the engagement, and the civilian population saw it only as a great blunder, the fighting forces of the Army of the Potomac kept their honor intact, despite the errors of General Ambrose E. Burnside.

In this book, certain limits have been imposed upon the scope of the material covered. In point of time, only the operations beginning with the assault crossing of the Rappahannock River by the Northern forces on December 11 and their withdrawal to the opposite bank five days later are reported in detail. However, in order to clarify the background of the battle, a short discussion of the events leading up to the combat has been included. The tactical and strategic details of the operation have been emphasized, since they best illustrate the problems of command.[1] Logistical and technical problems were included only when they had a direct influence on tactical decisions.

Although primary emphasis has been placed upon the Army of the Potomac, Confederate operations, when they throw light on Union activities, have also been included.

Two works dealing with the Battle of Fredericksburg were written prior to 1900 by George F. R. Henderson and Francis W. Palfrey.[2] In 1891 Henderson, in *The Campaign of Fredericksburg*, told the story of the battle primarily from the Confederate point of view. His purpose was to detail the lessons of the operation as they applied to the militia forces of the Great Britain of his day. Although the account

---

1. See Appendix C.
2. For a general bibliography, see pp. 139-47.

was well written and easy to follow, many of the conclusions have been outmoded by subsequent developments in tactics and weapons. Palfrey's volume, *The Antietam and Fredericksburg*, in the famous Scribner's "Campaigns of the Civil War," was completed in 1882, before many source materials had become generally available. However, on the whole, it is accurate and clearly written.

In 1906 Major G. W. Redway of the British Army wrote a study of the battle entitled *Fredericksburg*, which was published as the third volume of the "Special Campaign Series." Although he used the newly issued *Official Records* as a source, Redway studied the campaign in order to learn tactical lessons applicable to military operations of his time. Major John W. McDonald completed an unpublished manuscript on *The Battle of Fredericksburg* as a project of the Command and General Staff College in the 1930's. This work is quite detailed and consists almost entirely of material taken from the *Official Records*, resulting in an imbalance of source material. The manuscript is now on file at the Fredericksburg and Spotsylvania National Military Park at Fredericksburg, Virginia. The most recent secondary work on this subject was published in 1957 under the title *Drama on the Rappahannock: The Fredericksburg Campaign*. Edward J. Stackpole completed the book as the first of a series to be written on the Civil War campaigns which took place on the Rappahannock River. Although handsomely illustrated, the minor errors it contains somewhat impair its value. Its chief importance lies in the large number of pictorial aids. A biography of General Burnside by Ben: Perley Poore, published in 1882, touches only briefly on the Fredericksburg Campaign. It is highly laudatory in tone and contains factual errors which make it an unreliable source of information.

The secondary works cited above, with the exception of Poore's biography of the Union general, are factually accurate as far as they go, but they are not sufficiently detailed in their treatment of the Fredericksburg operation and are out of date in interpretation. Since the writers tended to concentrate on the military techniques of the battle which were still applicable to the battlefields of their own day, time has rendered their work obsolete.

The most important single source available to students of Civil War military campaigns is found in the *Official Records of the Union and Confederate Armies*. This massive set includes 128 volumes of records and an additional three-volume set of atlases. The *Official Records* includes the official reports of commanders at all levels and correspondence pertaining to military operations, both written and telegraphic. [In using this source caution is necessary because the reports were often written in a defensive tone after the actions described were over. The correspondence, however, was usually written while operations were in progress and therefore is more reliable.] *Battles and Leaders of the Civil War* is also a valuable source for contemporary accounts. The series consists of individual articles written by eyewitnesses of each of the important Civil War battles. In many cases these authors were the principal commanders on each side and therefore were in a position to give many details not found in the *Official Records*. The chief danger in using this source is again the defensive attitude and the self-interest of many of the contributors. Another valuable source of material is provided by a large number of regimental histories, many written by men who had participated in the events they describe. Most of the remaining sources fall into the category of periodicals, diaries, memoirs, and published letters. A student of the military phases of the Civil War is more often embarrassed by too much material than by too little.

In addition to written materials, the battlefield itself is well preserved as a National Military Park. The writer spent three weeks there studying the terrain over which the battle was fought. He also used materials available in the library maintained by the Park Service. The research thus conducted materially assisted him in the preparation of this book.

As indicated before, there has been no study of the Fredericksburg Campaign which has utilized all the materials now available. These materials include many diaries, as well as collections of contemporary documents which have been published to satisfy the growing interest in Civil War subjects. Representative of these works are the following: Charles Minor Blackford, *Letters from Lee's Army;* William Andrew Fletcher, *Rebel Private Front and Rear;* Henry Steele Commager, ed., *The Blue and the Gray;* and J. Cutler Andrews, *The North Reports the Civil War.* By employing all accessible sources, the author hopes to make a critical analysis of the operation in terms of the leadership principles which were applied or ignored by the Union commanders.

CHAPTER I

THE ARMIES

The Army of the Potomac which Major General Ambrose E. Burnside took over from the departing Major General George B. McClellan on November 7, 1862, consisted of 120,281 officers and men.[1] The troops were organized into six army corps of three divisions each. Although a division generally consisted of three brigades, Brigadier General Abner Doubleday's division of the First Corps had four brigades, while two of the divisions under Major General Joseph Hooker had only two brigades. In the Union army, a brigade was composed of three to six regiments, depending on their individual strength. When a regiment dwindled to a certain point, the unit was deactivated and a new regiment was organized. This system prevented new recruits from serving with combat veterans and benefiting from their experience. It also accounted for the variable number of regiments in each brigade.

Artillery was divided among the divisions in the army, which were allotted an average of four batteries of six field guns each to support their activities. The principle of concentrating supporting arms had not been accepted at this time; and, despite the excellence of the the Federal artillery, it was not fully utilized because of the splintering effect of this type of organization. The cavalry consisted of three separate brigades under the direct supervision of the commanding general. The technical services were grouped into separate units of appropriate size which received orders directly from army headquarters.[2]

When Burnside assumed command, he reorganized the army into three grand divisions, each consisting of two army corps plus one cavalry brigade. The Right Grand Division, commanded by Major General Edwin V. Sumner, included the Second and Ninth Army Corps; the Center Grand Division under Major General Joseph Hooker consisted of the Third and Fifth Army Corps; and the Left Grand Division, composed of the First and Sixth Army Corps, was commanded by Major General William B. Franklin. It should be noted that the cavalry, like the artillery, was distributed among component parts of

1

the army, precluding efficient use of that unit.[3] The grand division organization proved unwieldy except when the army operated in columns along separate routes. One more headquarters had been placed between the commanding general and the divisions which were his basic maneuver elements. The size of this new unit also proved too large to be used entirely as a reserve force, and in the coming battle one of the grand divisions was, in effect, never used as a unit but was broken up to provide reinforcements for the other two grand divisions. The position of the commander of this grand division was weakened because when he was finally committed to battle, most of his troops were already operating under the orders of the other grand divisions.[4] Although they were never on the field of battle at Fredericksburg, the Eleventh Army Corps under Major General Franz Sigel and the Twelfth Army Corps under Major General Henry W. Slocum were considered available as reinforcements to the main army. With the Twelfth Corps at Harpers Ferry and the Eleventh Corps in the vicinity of Warrenton, these troops were between the main army and Washington. Technically they were under the orders of General Burnside and toward the end of the battle were drawn closer to the operational area; but since they did not have any effect on the battle, they will not be considered further.[5]

On December 10, 1862, the Army of Northern Virginia reported 78,513 men present for duty.[6] Like Burnside, General Robert E. Lee had also reorganized his army just prior to the beginning of the campaign. On October 11, 1862, he grouped his army into two corps: the First Corps commanded by Lieutenant General James Longstreet and the Second Corps under Lieutenant General Thomas J. Jackson.[7] General Longstreet had five divisions with a total strength of twenty infantry brigades, while General Jackson's Corps contained four divisions with a total of nineteen infantry brigades. In the Confederate army all the major units were named after their commanders, as, for example, "Cobb's Brigade." This leads to some confusion in instances where commanders were either killed or transferred, since usually the name of the unit was not changed. Therefore, in the interest of clarity, the names of both the unit and its actual commander will be given.

The cavalry, composed of three brigades and a battalion of horse artillery, was centralized in one division under Major General James E. B. Stuart. One of the chief reasons for the effectiveness of the Confederate cavalry was its organization. General Stuart, with the aid of Major John Pelham's horse guns, utilized his force of almost ten thousand troopers to maximum advantage at the points of decision. General Lee kept central control of his cavalry so that it could be employed to the best advantage, and during the Fredericksburg fighting[8] there was a strong contrast between the relative effectiveness of the Confederate and the Union cavalry.

The artillery was partially divided among the divisions as in the Union army and partially consolidated under central control. Each division had two to six batteries permanently assigned for its own support. In addition, each corps commander retained certain batteries in reserve to be used anywhere along the corps front. The First Corps had ten batteries formed into two reserve battalions, and the Second Corps retained one reserve battalion of six batteries. General Lee also kept two reserve battalions of artillery, totaling eight batteries, for his own needs. This centralized use of the 279 guns of all types possessed by the Army of Northern Virginia proved efficient and increased the effectiveness of the Southern firepower.[9] In matériel, the Confederates were at a distinct disadvantage; most of their batteries contained several different types of artillery, multiplying the problems of the artillery commanders.

The infantry brigades varied in strength from three to six regiments; and except for a very few cases, all the troops in a brigade were from the same state. The replacement system used by the South was designed to keep each unit up to authorized strength by sending individual replacements to make up battle losses. Conscription helped insure a steady flow of men to the army, and most Confederate organizations were able to maintain their strength at acceptable levels during this period of the war.

CHAPTER II

THE ANTAGONISTS

Much of the story of Fredericksburg lies in the men who commanded the armies which came to grips during that damp, cold, foggy week in mid-December, 1862. The chief commanders on both sides had risen to positions of leadership because of their exemplary conduct in early battles of the Civil War. A brief sketch of these commanders may throw some light on their relative qualifications and help explain their behavior and attitudes toward the events which transpired on the Rappahannock's steep banks.

MAJOR GENERAL AMBROSE EVERETT BURNSIDE,
Commanding General, Army of the Potomac

Ambrose E. Burnside was born and raised in Indiana. At the time he assumed command, he was thirty-eight years old. He came from a large family, and when he was eighteen his father withdrew him from school and apprenticed him to be a tailor. Within a year, young Burnside was in business for himself, but in 1843 he abandoned commerce to accept an appointment to the United States Military Academy. In 1847 he graduated eighteenth in a class of thirty-eight, and was sent to Mexico as a second lieutenant of artillery. The Mexican War ended, however, before he could get to the front. The next six years were spent in assignments on the frontier and at Fort Adams, Rhode Island.

During the tour of duty on the frontier Burnside had seen the need for a breech-loading rifle for cavalrymen, and he perfected such a weapon while on duty in Rhode Island. Some of his friends encouraged him to leave the army in order to engage in the manufacture of his invention. Heeding their advice, Burnside resigned his commission in 1853 and set up a factory in Newport, Rhode Island, to manufacture the carbine. Apparently there had been an understanding between the War Department and Burnside, who assumed that his carbine would be purchased for army use. But when the factory was ready to produce, the contract was awarded to another firm, leaving

Burnside's company bankrupt. In 1858, attempting to recover his losses, he went to work for the Illinois Central Railroad. For a time he lived with George B. McClellan who was vice-president of the line. By hard work and personal sacrifice Burnside was able to liquidate all his debts before the Civil War began.

In 1861, he was living in Rhode Island, where he was appointed the commanding officer of the First Rhode Island Regiment, one of the earliest units to arrive in Washington after the outbreak of hostilities. His martial appearance and well-disciplined regiment won him command of a brigade of volunteers at the Battle of Bull Run. The brigade took a prominent part in the flanking attack in this battle, although some officers felt Burnside had been slow in moving to the attack.

Commissioned a brigadier general of volunteers in August 1861, he was assigned to command a division of New England troops which took part in an amphibious assault on New Bern, North Carolina, in January of 1862. This expedition confirmed Burnside's military reputation. Although the enemy was greatly outnumbered and did not call upon Burnside to employ more than the simplest military skill, his victory won him the stars of a major general of volunteers and command of the reinforcements for the Army of the Potomac during the Second Manassas Campaign. He commanded the right wing of the army at the Battle of South Mountain and the left wing at the Battle of Antietam. At Antietam his military performance left much to be desired; and General McClellan, at least privately, held him responsible for the indecisiveness of the victory. His chief faults seemed to be a lack of energy when action was required and an excess of boldness when prudence was called for.

Burnside was the prototype of a perfect major general, and his likeable personal traits earned him many friends. A revealing picture of his character is painted by one of his military subordinates, Major General Jacob D. Cox, whose description of Burnside follows:

> In the afternoon I met Burnside for the first time, and was warmly attracted by him, as everyone was. He was pre-eminently a manly man, as I expressed it in writing home. His large, fine eyes, his winning smile and cordial manners bespoke a frank, sincere and honorable character, and these indications were never belied by more intimate acquaintance. . . . I learned to understand the limitations of his powers and the points in which he fell short of being a great commander; but as I knew him better, I estimated

more and more highly his sincerity and truthfulness, his unselfish generosity, and his devoted patriotism. In everything which makes up an honorable and lovable character he had no superior.[1]

This is the description of a man who might be sought for a friend, but it is not the prescription for a great commander. Burnside seemed to affect everyone he met in this way, and it is unfortunate that he combined such a winning personality with a great lack of talent for military command. The man's very honesty would not allow him to pretend to talent he did not possess. At every opportunity he tried to tell his superiors that he lacked the capacity to command a large army. But with his other virtues so obvious, President Abraham Lincoln probably thought Burnside's protestations were prompted by modesty. When he was finally prevailed upon to take command, after emphatically attempting to turn it down for the third time, he seems to have lapsed into a severe depression. Brigadier General Oliver O. Howard described Burnside's appearance two days after his appointment in this way:

> Soon after this interview I met Burnside, who appeared sad and weary. He had been for two nights almost without sleep. He remarked in my presence that he had concluded to take the command of the army, but did not regard the subject as one for congratulation.[2]

Thus at the beginning of a difficult winter campaign in hostile territory, against a military genius of the first order, the Army of the Potomac was led by a well-meaning general only too aware of his own deficiencies.[3]

When the Army of the Potomac was reorganized into grand divisions, General Burnside elevated three of his major generals from corps commands to assume control of the larger units. These men were to play leading roles in the battle to come.

MAJOR GENERAL EDWIN VOSE SUMNER,
Commanding General, Right Grand Division

General Sumner was born in Boston in 1797, and at the age of sixty-five was the oldest major commander on the field. He entered the regular service as a second lieutenant of infantry in 1819 and remained in the army until shortly before his death in 1863. As a captain of dragoons he served on the frontier and at the beginning of the Mexican War was major of the Second Dragoons. He had a distinguished combat record as a regimental commander with General

Winfield Scott's army in the drive to Mexico City, having been wounded and twice breveted for bravery in action during this campaign.

After the war, Sumner reverted to the rank of lieutenant colonel in the Second Dragoons and again served on the frontier. A full colonel by 1855, he was given command of Fort Leavenworth, Kansas, at the time of the Free Soil disturbances in that state. Charged with pro-slavery sympathies, General Sumner nevertheless maintained order by disarming and dispersing raiding bands of both persuasions. He had no sympathy for the doctrine of secession and staunchly supported the Union. Well-liked by General Scott, who was the General-in-Chief at the time, Sumner was chosen to accompany President-elect Abraham Lincoln to Washington for his inauguration in 1861.

With the opening of hostilities, Sumner was commissioned a brigadier general of volunteers and served as a brigade commander at Bull Run. His brigade of volunteers behaved poorly, but his own conduct was rewarded by elevation to the command of the Second Army Corps. He led this corps during the Peninsula Campaign and at South Mountain and Antietam. He was promoted to major general of volunteers on July 4, following the Seven Days Battle on the Peninsula. Although personally brave, his record as a senior commander was spotty, with some indications that he lost control of the situation in the heat of combat.

General Sumner was an energetic and brave officer, well-imbued with the spirit of offensive. He tended, however, to be more the capable soldier than competent commander once the shooting started. Burnside chose Sumner from the three grand division commanders to be with him throughout the battle and consulted with him about orders he issued during the fighting.[4]

MAJOR GENERAL JOSEPH HOOKER,
Commanding General, Center Grand Division

General Hooker, another Massachusetts man, was born in 1814 at Hadley. After completing his preparatory education at Hopkins Academy, he received an appointment to the United States Military Academy in 1833. Four years later he graduated as number twenty-nine in a class of fifty, and soon afterwards was assigned to a short tour of duty in Florida during the Indian uprisings there. He served as the adjutant of the Military Academy and of the First Artillery prior to the Mexican War, during which he held staff appointments under Generals

Zachary Taylor and Winfield Scott. In those days staff assignment did not inhibit a soldier from engaging in combat, and General Hooker quickly distinguished himself by repeated examples of bravery in the field. He was breveted captain for gallantry at Monterey, major for bravery at the Battle of National Bridge, and lieutenant colonel for his performance at Chapultepec.

While serving on the staff of General Gideon J. Pillow, he became embroiled in a controversy between his superior and General Scott. This controversy and his realization of the lack of opportunity in the peacetime army caused Hooker to resign his commission in 1853. He moved to California and for five years was a farmer at Sonoma. He served a short tour as Superintendent of Military Roads in Oregon and then returned to California to assist in the formation of a militia regiment. When the Civil War began Hooker offered his services to the government and went to Washington to await his appointment to duty. His first important command, after being commissioned a briga-dier general in May, 1861, was a division in the Peninsula Campaign. The unit particularly distinguished itself at Williamsburg and in the Seven Days Battle. As a result of his impetuous gallantry in combat, which, on occasion, led him to reckless commitment of his unit, Hook-er won the sobriquet of "Fighting Joe" and the command of the First Army Corps. He commanded the corps during the Maryland Cam-paign and was wounded at Antietam. Although Hooker was a hard fighter, he lacked the talent for independent command, a fact well demonstrated the following summer at Chancellorsville.

Tall, robust, and affable, Joe Hooker's ego led him to expound his opinions of other officers' shortcomings and he proved to be a dis-ruptive influence in Burnside's army. Hooker wanted the top com-mand position for himself and schemed to get it. General Burnside did not like Hooker personally, and Hooker's outspoken criticism of Burnside's blunders antagonized him further. A major general in September, 1862, "Fighting Joe" lived up to his nickname during the Battle of Fredericksburg but he never supported the commanding general with his full cooperation.[5]

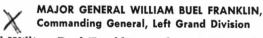

MAJOR GENERAL WILLIAM BUEL FRANKLIN,
Commanding General, Left Grand Division

General William Buel Franklin was born in Pennsylvania. His father, who was active in state politics, procured his appointment to West Point in 1839. Franklin graduated in 1843, first in his class. He selected service in the topographical engineers, at that time a separate branch of the army. After service on the survey teams which mapped the Great Lakes area, he was sent on similar expeditions along the frontier. When the Mexican War began he was attached to General Taylor's command and was present at the Battle of Buena Vista. Following the war, he engaged in peacetime army assignments and was promoted to captain in 1857. One of his most important assignments was as engineer in charge of constructing the dome on the Capitol Building in Washington. Thirty-eight years old at the start of the Civil War, Franklin was commissioned brigadier general of volunteers and commanded a brigade at the Battle of Bull Run. His brigade did not distinguish itself, but considering the material he had to work with, Franklin did a good job. He was given command of a division at the beginning of the Peninsula Campaign, and in May of that year was promoted to command the Sixth Army Corps. Leading his corps through the remainder of the fighting on the Peninsula and the Antietam Campaign, he earned the respect if not the admiration of contemporaries for his military skill. He was promoted to major general in July shortly before fighting on the Peninsula ceased. General Franklin had a reputation as an excellent corps commander, well-grounded in his profession, and it was his grand division which was selected to make the main attack at Fredericksburg.[6]

These were the men who directed the Army of the Potomac as it massed along the north bank of the Rappahannock River preparatory to testing once again the strength of the Army of Northern Virginia.

The Confederate Army was directed by a triumvirate of extraordinary commanders. These three men had by December 1862 perfected their tactical teamwork. General Robert E. Lee had promoted Lieutenant General Thomas J. Jackson and Lieutenant General James Longstreet to the command of the two newly organized army corps which made up his Army of Northern Virginia. The success of the attempt to halt an offensive thrust of the Union army was to depend to a large extent on the capabilities of these three men.

GENERAL ROBERT EDWARD LEE,
Commanding General, Army of Northern Virginia

Robert E. Lee, the fifth child of the Revolutionary War hero, Henry "Light Horse Harry" Lee, was born in January 1807. Raised at "Stratford," the ancestral home in Virginia, and educated in the schools of

Alexandria, young Lee entered the United States Military Academy in 1825. A superior student, he graduated from the Academy second in his class in 1829. He selected service in the topographical engineers and spent the next seventeen years in peacetime engineering assignments. Much of this time was spent on the construction of Atlantic Coast fortifications and harbor improvements. During the Mexican War he served with General John E. Wool for a short time, then was transferred to General Scott's command for the Mexico City Campaign. His excellent reconnaissance work at Cerro Gordo, Churubusco, and Chapultepec contributed to the success of American operations and he was breveted colonel. Following the war, he served a term as Superintendent of the Military Academy and another as lieutenant colonel of the Second Cavalry. His frontier service with the cavalry was interrupted by family problems that kept him moving back and forth from Virginia to his regiment on the frontier.

Lee was in Washington when news of the John Brown raid reached the War Department. He was dispatched to restore order and accomplished this mission with a minimum loss of life. At the beginning of the Civil War, he was unofficially offered the field command of the United States Army, but he decided that his first loyalty lay with his state and resigned his Federal commission.

Lee's first military effort for the Confederacy was directing the unsuccessful West Virginia campaign, which did much to lower his popular reputation. He received his commission as general in August, 1861, and was sent to superintend the construction of harbor defenses on the South Atlantic coast line. That assignment completed he returned to Richmond as military advisor to the Confederate President. In this rather anomalous position, he acted as intermediary between President Jefferson Davis and General Joseph E. Johnston, the commander of the field army in Virginia. When General Johnston was wounded, in August 1862, Lee assumed command of the troops defending Richmond. He rapidly launched a series of offensives against General McClellan's forces which, although tactically not very successful, were strategically effective. With the pressure on the capital relieved, Lee then moved against Major General John Pope and his Federal Army of Virginia. These forces were defeated at Second Bull Run and driven in confusion back to Washington. Victory over Pope was followed by the indecisive Maryland Campaign during which Lee's forces were badly mauled, and he barely managed to get away from Antietam with his army intact. Notwithstanding the reverse at

Antietam, General Lee had established and sustained moral ascendancy over his Federal opponents. He had already become a myth of invincibility to his Southern soldiery. Lee was more than a match for Burnside; and although the defender can only react to the attacker, few flaws can be found in the Southerner's tactical conduct of the defensive battle.[7]

LIEUTENANT GENERAL JAMES LONGSTREET,
Commanding General, First Corps

James Longstreet was born in Edgefield, South Carolina, in 1821 and was raised in Georgia and Alabama. He entered West Point as a member of the class of 1842, along with Ulysses S. Grant, Henry Halleck, and William T. Sherman. Graduating only fifty-fourth in a class of sixty-two, he was assigned as second lieutenant of infantry in the Fourth Regiment. A tour of duty fighting Indians in Florida occupied the young lieutenant until the beginning of the Mexican War. He fought with General Taylor at Monterey and then was reassigned to Scott's army where he fought throughout the campaign to take Mexico City. He was wounded at Chapultepec and breveted major for his gallantry in that action. Transferred to the paymaster corps after the Mexican War, he was finally promoted to major in 1861.

Longstreet went south at the start of the Civil War, hoping to get a commission in the Confederate paymaster corps; instead, his good reputation in the "old Army" won him a commission as a brigadier general. His fine battle performance as a brigade commander at the Battle of Bull Run was rewarded with major general's stars in October of 1861. Longstreet served as a division commander on the Peninsula during the defense of Richmond and then under Lee at the Battle of the Seven Days, Second Bull Run, and the Maryland Campaign. Lee appointed Longstreet commander of the First Corps, and he achieved the rank of lieutenant general on the eleventh of October, 1862.

Longstreet was a fine corps commander, particularly cool in combat. His subordinates marvelled at his stamina and his grasp of a tactical situation. He was especially fond of the defensive battle and was at his very best when fighting from a position he had had time to prepare. It was this officer's portion of the front which bore the brunt of the assaults from the Federal Right Grand Division and inflicted the heaviest losses upon the attacking regiments.[8]

11

LIEUTENANT GENERAL THOMAS JONATHAN JACKSON,
Commanding General, Second Corps

Thomas J. Jackson was born of very poor parents in Clarksburg, Virginia, in 1824. His parents died when he was young, and he was raised by an uncle who could not afford to provide him with a very sound education. He received an appointment to the United States Military Academy in 1842, and by tremendous effort and long hours of extra study he overcame the handicap of his poor education to graduate seventeenth in a class of fifty-nine.

Immediately after graduation he was sent to the war in Mexico where he soon distinguished himself under fire. Ordinarily a taciturn personality, Jackson seemed to blossom under combat conditions. He was noticed by his superiors for his actions at Vera Cruz, Cerro Gordo, and Chapultepec, for which he was breveted major within eighteen months after graduation from the Military Academy. Four years after the end of the Mexican War, he left the army to accept a position as professor of artillery tactics and natural philosophy at the Virginia Military Institute. His term as a professor was not especially successful; and, although his private life was happy, his many eccentricities led the cadets to call him "Mad Tom" Jackson.

During the John Brown raid at Harpers Ferry, Jackson commanded a cadet corps called out to assist in putting down the raiders and was present at the execution of the abolitionist martyr. His name was presented for consideration for a command in the Confederate army, but he was so little known that only a commission as colonel was secured for him. His first duty was organizing a regiment at Harpers Ferry, for which his experience had prepared him. In command of a brigade of infantry at the Battle of Bull Run, his sturdy defense of Henry House Hill helped win the victory for the South and also gave him his immortal *nom de guerre*, "Stonewall." He was promoted to major general in October, 1861, and placed in command of forces in the Shenandoah Valley. During the period of March through April 1862, Jackson, under Lee's direction, conducted his famous Valley Campaign, one of the most perfect operations in American military history. His now-famous "foot cavalry" next participated in the Seven Days Campaign, but here Jackson did not distinguish himself. He did, however, play a major role in the Second Bull Run Campaign and during the Maryland Campaign.

Jackson was most often used by Lee as the maneuver force during envelopments of his opponents' flanks, and he operated well with a minimum of supervision. The two rebel commanders worked together harmoniously, and Jackson was able to implement Lee's strategic conceptions to perfection. When employed in the defensive, Jackson was always eager for the riposte and followed it up by relentless pursuit. It was on his portion of the line that the only Conferedate counter-attack was launched during the entire battle of Fredericksburg. [9]

The Conferedate command — composed of Lee, Longstreet, and Jackson — was probably the finest set of battle leaders serving during the entire Civil War. They directed an army high in morale and strong in numbers and experience.

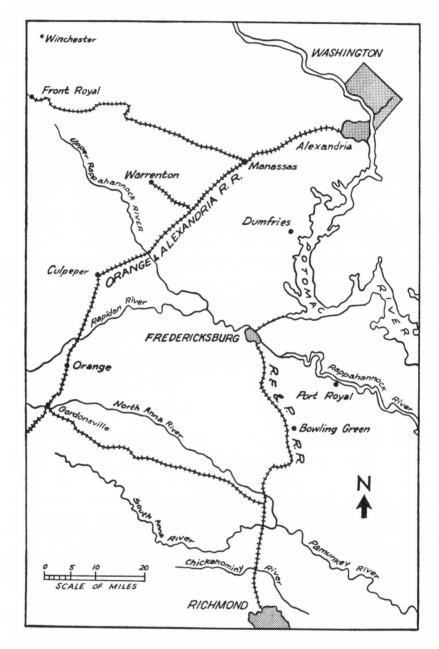

MAP 1 — Virginia Theater of Operations
Based on Highway Map of State of Virginia, 1956.

CHAPTER III

ANTIETAM AND AFTER

In order to understand fully events occurring in the Fredericksburg operations, it is necessary to take into account certain events which preceded them. During the previous September, the Battle of South Mountain and Antietam had brought Lee's first invasion of the North to an unsuccessful conclusion. General McClellan chose to keep his Army of the Potomac north of the Potomac River for rest and re-supply, which also allowed the badly battered Army of Northern Virginia an opportunity for respite and replenishment. Civilian authorities in Washington were eager, however, for an immediate pursuit of the Confederates in order to reap the benefits of the Antietam victory. President Lincoln had been dissatisfied with the offensive efforts of General McClellan and was urging him to press forward while the good weather held. Finally, on October 26, 1862, McClellan started across the Potomac, moving east of the Blue Ridge Mountains and protecting his right flank by seizing gaps in that range as he proceeded south.

By November 7, the main strength of the Union army was concentrated in the vicinity of Warrenton, Virginia, on the Orange and Alexandria Railroad. General Lee had divided his army, bivouacking the Second Corps near Winchester in the Shenandoah Valley, while the First Corps was blocking the further advance of the Federals at Culpeper Court House. McClellan hoped to strike Lee's army while it was separated and defeat Lee piecemeal, but he never had the opportunity to test the success of his plan, since the President chose that particular moment to relieve McClellan from command and replace him with Major General Ambrose E. Burnside.[1]

Brigadier General Catharinus P. Buckingham of the staff of the War Department was dispatched with the orders relieving McClellan and appointing Burnside his successor. General Buckingham arrived at the Army of the Potomac's railhead early in the evening of November 7 and set off through a snowstorm to find Ninth Corps Headquarters. He presented himself to General Burnside about eleven o'clock that night and gave him both orders. At first Burnside seemed to be in a state of shock. The orders were completely unexpected, particularly with the army in the middle of a campaign. On two previous occasions the command had been offered to him, but he had vehemently refused even to consider accepting it. He told General Buckingham that he did not have the capacity for handling such a large military organization and did not want the job. After discussing the matter with two of his staff officers for almost two hours, he finally consented to assume the command, especially since the President was in fact giving him an order which he, as a soldier, could not disobey. Some officers later expressed the opinion that he was also influenced by a fear that if he did not accept the command it would be offered to General Hooker.[2]

Burnside and Buckingham then went over to McClellan's headquarters to inform him of his relief. Unknown to them, General McClellan had already received a report of the arrival of General Buckingham and had noted the fact that Buckingham had reported first to Burnside rather than to him, as would have been customary. He was alone in his tent writing a letter to his wife when the two men arrived. After inviting them in, he engaged them in small talk for a few minutes before inquiring the purpose of their late evening visit. Actually he had little doubt of their purpose, for apparently he had suspected that he might be removed as a result of his lack of rapport with the military and civil authorities in Washington. Finally the order for his relief was presented to him, and he immediately told Burnside that he turned the command over to him along with congratulations. He tried to make Burnside feel better about the change by reminding him that he had to take over, for the order of relief must be obeyed.[3] McClellan made every effort to facilitate the changeover and to familiarize Burnside with the situation of the army.

Although McClellan was absolutely correct and courteous to Burnside, he did not hold a high opinion of his successor's military powers. He felt that Burnside was culpable for having failed to strike swiftly when the opportunity still existed for overwhelming victory at Antietam. In a letter to his wife, following the battle, he indicated that, "I ought to treat Burnside *very* severely, and probably will; yet I hate to do it. He is very slow; is not fit to command more than a regiment."[4] This opinion, while not widespread in the army at this time, was shared by many of the senior officers. Prepared as they were to give Burnside their cooperation, they had misgivings about the future employment of the army.

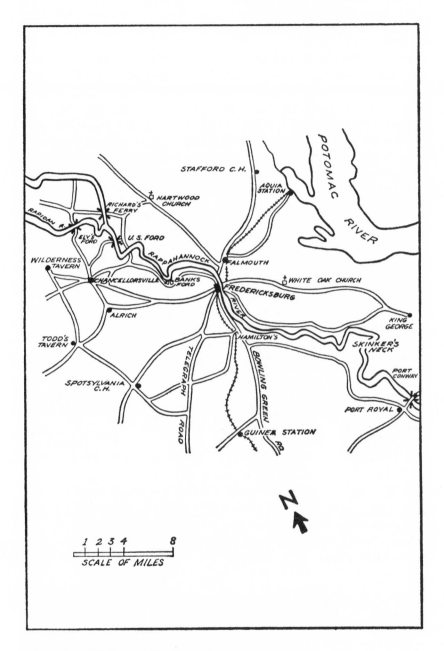

MAP 2 — Valley of the Rappahannock
Based on map, Stackpole, *The Fredericksburg Campaign*, p. 105.

The unexpected news of General McClellan's retirement from active command took the army by surprise. He was idolized by the men, and many emotional scenes were enacted during his few remaining days with the army. There was some talk of marching on Washington to rectify the supposed injustice and this gave the impression that morale in the army was much worse than it actually was. Majority opinion supported a wait-and-see attitude which would give Burnside a chance to prove himself a fit successor to "Little Mac." When the news reached General Lee, he facetiously remarked that he was sorry to see McClellan go, since he understood him so well. As it turned out, the change proved to be all in Lee's favor.

General Burnside quickly took the reins of power. With a make-shift staff, he began to plan a course of action. He checked the forward momentum of his troops which, according to McClellan's original scheme, were concentrated around Warrenton, and proceeded to develop a campaign plan completely different from the one the army had been following.

Under the terms of the order appointing him commander of the Army of the Potomac, Burnside was to report his plans for the movement of the army to Major General Henry W. Halleck, the General-in-Chief, immediately. On November 9, after discussing the matter with his staff and chief subordinates, he submitted a plan to shift his line of operations from the Orange and Alexandria Railroad to the Richmond, Fredericksburg, and Potomac Railroad line. Adoption of this course would have meant abandoning gains made by the campaign then in progress and also wasting considerable logistic matériel expended to provide a supply line for the movement south along the Orange and Alexandria. His reasoning was based on a desire to surprise Lee and also to minimize logistic problems posed by a winter campaign with a large army in a hostile country. The primitive condition of Virginia roads left the Union army tied to its rail lines as far as overland supply was concerned, since bad weather easily turned these roads into quagmires impassable to wagon trains. The basic strategy would have consisted of a feint toward Culpeper and Gordonsville, followed by a rapid shift to the Rappahannock at Fredericksburg, and from there swift movement to Richmond before the Confederates could unite their divided forces and intervene.[5]

The great objective of the campaign was to have been the capture of Richmond, not destruction of the Confederate army. This preoccupation with the capture of Richmond has since been criticized frequently as a violation of the rule of war decreeing destruction of an enemy's military forces as the primary objective. The capture of Richmond by the Federal forces would have been a victory of major importance for the North because of industrial concentration in that city, in addition to its psychological value as the Confederate capital. Such facilities as the Tredagar Iron Works and many other war industries in Richmond made it a prime strategic as well as political target. Any Union army seriously threatening the Confederate capital would draw the Confederate army like a magnet and if the movement were swift enough, that army might have to fight from a disadvantageous position.

Throughout the entire war in the East the Union army had to keep in mind that in addition to an offensive mission it had defensive responsibilities. The national capital had to be protected at all times, and the civilian leaders were particularly interested in any plan that might promise the capture of Richmond and at the same time safeguard Washington. Burnside's plan attempted to provide for accomplishment of both missions. There were however several inherent difficulties in the Fredericksburg route. By moving to this line, a number of defensive obstacles were placed directly in the path of Burnside's army. Beyond the Rappahannock, the North and South Anna and the Chickahominy Rivers remained athwart the road to Richmond. Even if initially successful, Burnside would have been faced with the unpleasant prospect of trying to force a series of easily defended river lines; and, even having achieved these crossings, he would have been met by Rebels firmly intrenched in strong fortifications around Richmond.

The advantages of the plan, however, were considerable and important. The shortest overland route from Washington to Richmond lay in proceeding from Fredericksburg directly south to the Confederate capital, and the supply route was completely secure from Washington to Fredericksburg via the Potomac River controlled by Union naval power. The supply of the Army of the Potomac in winter over the shorter railroad line starting at Aquia Creek Landing and running south through Fredericksburg to Richmond would have been much safer than over the longer Orange and Alexandria line. By following the Fredericksburg line, the Union army would also have been between the Confederate army and Washington throughout the push southwards.

The Rappahannock south of Fredericksburg was not fordable by large bodies of troops. Burnside therefore requested authorities in

Washington to send pontoon trains and supplies to meet his army when it arrived from Warrenton. He wanted sufficient bridging for two pontoon tracks across the river so the army could cross as quickly as possible. Once the army arrived at Falmouth, on the East side of the Rappahannock across from Fredericksburg, General Lee would certainly launch countermeasures. Therefore, if the maximum advantage were to be gained from the change of lines, the move south from the river would have to be rapid. In order to keep Lee from determining the real objective of the Union advance for as long as possible, Burnside's cavalry and pickets were to make a feint towards Culpeper in an attempt to divert Confederates to the defense of that line until it was too late to interfere with the real move. A final recommendation favoring the change in campaign plan was that if the Federals ran into trouble or bad weather, they would be in a better position to extricate themselves because of their more secure line of retreat. [6]

This plan was forwarded to General Halleck, who immediately requested a conference with General Burnside. Because the proposed plan involved the logistical-support commands, Halleck brought with him Quartermaster General Montgomery C. Meigs and Brigadier General Herman Haupt, commander of the Military Railroad. At a meeting held in Warrenton on November 12 and 13, General Halleck attempted to dissuade Burnside from the shift of bases and encouraged him to continue the movement toward Culpeper and Gordonsville. It should be noted that the General-in-Chief did not assume operational control of the armies in the field; his function was to advise the President on military matters. In questions of strategy, the President's concurrence was necessary; however, during Halleck's term of office, many of the major decisions were actually made by President Lincoln.

General Burnside continued to advocate his own plan during the two-day conference. Finally, General Halleck declared that he would not be responsible for issuing an approval for the new plan, but would leave the final decision up to Lincoln. He told Burnside to go ahead with the planning for the new move, but not to put it into execution until he received notification from Washington.

Although this plan seemed clear enough at the time, during this conference a basic misunderstanding of the proposal somehow occurred between the two generals, a misunderstanding which was to have fatal consequences for the chance of success. General Burnside contemplated a swift thrust to Falmouth, which would place the unfordable portion of the Rapahannock directly in his path and make availability of bridging material vital to his plan. General Halleck, on the other hand, thought that Burnside was planning to cross Rappahannock fords north of the city and then march his army down the Confederate side of the river and seize the town and heights behind it from the flank. He asserted in his Annual Report for 1862 that the move actually performed by Burnside was never approved by either himself or the President.[7]

Exactly how this misunderstanding could have occurred is hard to understand, since both officers had held the conference in the presence of their staffs and General Burnside had gone to some lengths to insure that the pontoon bridging would be waiting at Falmouth when his troops arrived. General Halleck later used the following statement, issued by Burnside after the defeat, as proof that the plan approved by the President was not the one actually followed by Burnside:

> The fact that I decided to move from Warrenton onto this line rather against the opinion of the President, Secretary, and yourself, and that you have left the whole management in my hands, without giving me orders, makes me the more responsible.[8]

General Halleck's assumption does not seem very fair; it is obvious that Burnside was referring to the switch from the Orange and Alexandria Railroad to the Fredericksburg line. General Halleck also avers in his Annual Report for 1862 that there was a spoken agreement between the two officers which called for modification of the written plan, and re-routed the army down the south bank of the Rappahannock. Except for his own assertion, no evidence can be found to support General Halleck's contention. General Burnside reiterated in his report, completed in November 1865, that his plan called for the army to cross the Rappahannock at Fredericksburg on pontoon bridges supplied by the authorities in Washington.[9]

In determining the value of this shift in the axis of advance to the Fredericksburg line, the outcome of the campaign should not obscure the very real merits of Burnside's plan. His desire to provide a shorter and safer supply line for the army and to eliminate reliance on the overworked Orange and Alexandria Railroad was supported by General Haupt. He had delivered his opinion of the weakness of this artery in a letter to Burnside on November 9, 1862, in which he stated:

> The road by which your army is to be supplied is a single track, without sidings sufficient for long trains, without wood and with insufficient supply of water, a road which has heretofore failed

to supply an army of one-fourth the size of that which you command. . . . If you advance far, the operation of the road will present greater difficulty; its protection against raids will be almost impossible and the breaks of connection will become frequent from various causes not dependent on the movement of the enemy.[10]

In addition to the logistic advantages of the new axis of advance, the plan also contained some strategic merit. General Lee had countered the advance of General McClellan by splitting his army, leaving Lieutenant General Thomas "Stonewall" Jackson on the flank of the advancing Federal army. Jackson had concentrated his Second Corps in the vicinity of Winchester in the Shenandoah Valley and was prepared to attack the Union army's rear and supply line if opportunity offered. The farther south the Federals advanced, the more vulnerable they became to such a stroke. As long as General Burnside continued to operate on the Orange and Alexandria axis, this threat to his lengthening supply lines would tend to restrict his freedom. However, by side-stepping to the left and moving along the direct road to Richmond, he stood a good chance of getting there before the bulk of Lee's separated forces could muster to dispute his advance. Once Richmond was threatened, Confederate authorities doubtless would require Lee to make a direct defense of the capital, a necessity which would preclude any effective Confederate threat to Washington. This plan was similar in many respects to the series of flanking moves made by Lieutenant General Ulysses S. Grant during his final campaign of the war, a strategy which has brought him much high praise and a little criticism.

The only major alternative General Burnside could have chosen would have been to continue the advance on the same line McClellan had been following. McClellan insisted later that he was about to bring Lee to battle, and that only his removal prevented that denouement. That General McClellan actually would have been able to force Lee into action in the vicinity of Culpeper is highly doubtful, since Lee could have continued to retreat until Jackson rejoined the main army. The lateness of the season did not give the Union commander enough time for a winter flanking movement back to the Peninsula, even if the President had allowed such a move. Besides, the North was demanding an advance before winter set in and expected another trial at arms before the army went into winter quarters.

Considering these factors, General Burnside's blueprint for the campaign was essentially sound. It had one great weakness, however, which doomed the campaign almost before it had begun. If the plan were to succeed, the enemy had to be deceived up to the last possible moment, for once the movement was begun it had to be continued without interruption. In the final analysis, Burnside's plan foundered on his inability to execute it without a hitch.

PRELIMINARY MOVEMENTS TO FALMOUTH

Following the meeting with the General-in-Chief, Burnside completed staff work necessary to ready the plan for action. The concentration of troops near Warrenton was completed, while Quartermaster officers anticipated the shift by starting to move accumulated stores away from Warrenton. On November 14, Burnside received a telegram from General Halleck giving the President's approval of the plan. Lincoln had indicated to Halleck, however, that he thought the plan would succeed only if carried out rapidly.[11] Burnside tried his best to comply with the President's advice and move quickly. Preliminary planning had geared the army for a rapid march and, since the troops were in the middle of a campaign when the new orders were issued, they were ready to move on short notice.

Unfortunately, necessary logistic arrangements could not be completed with the same celerity. The Quartermaster General made every effort to speed rations and other supplies to Falmouth in time to support the movements of the army, but there was a total lack of terminal facilities at the Aquia Creek landing. A ten-mile stretch of rail line connected Aquia Creek landing and Fredericksburg via a bridge over the Rappahannock. This bridge, along with a large wharf and landing facilities at Aquia Creek, had been destroyed by the Federal army following Major General John Pope's disaster at Second Bull Run. Until these facilities could be replaced, major supply operations at that point were out of the question. Nor could the army cross the Rappahannock in any force without pontoon bridges, and these bridges were destined to arrive long after all hope of surprising the Confederate command had passed.

The tardy arrival of the pontoon bridging became one of the chief reasons advanced for the failure of the campaign and the loss of the battle. The bridging itself was under the control of the Engineer Brigade which had been ordered to move it from the depot in Washington to Falmouth. The matériel was supposed to be concentrated at the depot in the capital, but because of a delay in orders most of the available pontoons were still at Berlin, Maryland, where the Army of the Potomac had crossed into Virginia at the beginning of the campaign.[12] Burnside first learned of the possible delay on November 14 when an inquiry by his engineer officer elicited the information that the required pontoons and wagons were just then arriving in Washington. The engineers promised to forward the bridges as quickly as possible and indicated that they would be entrained by November 17 at the latest.

The troop movement had not yet begun, so Burnside could have suspended movement of the army until the bridging was available. He elected, however, to commence the march as scheduled, and the army began to move out in multiple columns on the morning of November 15. Major General Sumner left the Warrenton area first, taking his Right Grand Division along the direct road to Falmouth, which his advance elements reached on the evening of November 17. On November 16, Major General Franklin's Left Grand Division moved out of Warrenton. Franklin took the road to Stafford Court House and arrived there on the evening of November 18. Major General Hooker brought up the rear of the army with his Center Grand Division, arriving at Hartwood on November 19. Cavalry was posted to cover the fords of the Rappahannock beyond Hooker's position and the roads leading to the rear of the army. Strong cavalry pickets were placed on the line of the upper Rappahannock.

The rapid move had been accomplished; the troops moved the thirty-six miles from Warrenton in two days of fast marching. They were now concentrated within easy supporting distance of each other in the vicinity of Falmouth. When General Sumner arrived opposite Fredericksburg on November 17, his advance elements were fired upon by a small battery of Confederate artillery which was quickly silenced by the fire of a battery of ten-pounder Parrott guns commanded by Captain Rufus D. Pettit. Only small numbers of Confederate troops were observed on the opposite bank and to all appearances did not consist of more than a strong picket post. However, the pontoon bridges had not yet arrived from Washington. Poor organization and bad weather delayed their arrival until November 25.

Sumner, in view of the very light opposition, requested permission to send troops across the river via the fords just north of Fredericksburg and seize the high ground dominating the exits from the town. General Burnside refused to allow this move because of the precarious nature of the fords and the strong possibility that a heavy seasonal rainstorm might flood out the fords and strand the detachment. Until pontoon bridges could be emplaced, no forward movement across the river was possible without grave risks.[13]

General Hooker, upon his arrival at Hartwood, had requested permission to cross his entire command via the United States Ford and then strike southeast for Bowling Green. He argued that once there he could draw forage and subsistence from the country and other re-supply from Port Royal on the Rappahannock.[14] General Burnside refused to sanction this movement on the same grounds that he had refused Sumner. It was exasperating for the Union subordinate commanders to sit quietly by and watch the Confederates across the Rappahannock leisurely concentrating their forces. But a premature crossing could have resulted in piecemeal defeat. There is the possibility that, had strong forces crossed at United States Ford, the Confederates would have fallen back to the Anna Rivers and made their defense at that line. Without bridges or railroad, however, no real penetration past the Rappahannock was feasible. There is some evidence that at this time General Burnside did contemplate sending light forces of infantry, cavalry, and artillery over the fords to seize the town, in order to secure both river banks during construction of the bridges; but upon receiving reports of the continued delay of the pontoon trains, he decided not to allow any element of the army to cross until he had the means to cross successfully the main body.[15] The prudence of this decision was confirmed by a closer examination of the fords, which showed those at Falmouth to be impractical for any but mounted troops, while the Hartwood fords would have required temporary bridging to expedite a mass crossing by troops.

The long overdue pontoon trains finally arrived on November 25, after being towed by water from Washington to Aquia Creek and thence overland. It had been Burnside's intention to cross the Rappahannock as soon as the bridges arrived and could be assembled, but the delay had allowed the Confederates time to concentrate at Fredericksburg for defense of the town. Therefore, Burnside was faced with an essentially new strategic problem, and he deferred action until all logistic preparations could be completed.

LEE CONCENTRATES HIS FORCES

When the news of General McClellan's relief reached the Confederate headquarters, followed by the halt of the Union advance, General Lee realized that a change in Union plans must be in the offing. He felt that the dispositions he had made to frustrate the move on Culpeper and Gordonsville had been successful. Forced by lack of strength to be on the defensive, he calmly waited to see what Burnside's first move would be. At this time a small force consisting of the Fifteenth Virginia Cavalry, four companies of Mississippi infantry, and a light battery of artillery was stationed at Fredericksburg to prevent any crossing at that point by light Union forces. It was this unit which fired on General Sumner's advance elements on November 17; and, despite the Confederate claims after the battle, it could not have interfered seriously with any Union crossing. General Lee was informed on the seventeenth of the movements of Sumner's column toward Falmouth and also of the arrival of Federal transports and gunboats at Aquia Creek on November 15, leading him to believe that Fredericksburg was to be reoccupied and made the base for a new drive on Richmond. He immediately ordered Major General Lafayette McLaws' and Brigadier General Robert Ransom's divisions, with a brigade of cavalry under Brigadier General William H. F. Lee, to reinforce the garrison at Fredericksburg.

To determine more fully the intentions of his enemy, Lee ordered Major General James E. B. Stuart to cross the Rappahannock at Warrenton Springs and collect intelligence. Stuart forced a crossing on November 18, dispersing a regiment of Federal cavalry which was guarding the ford, and rode into Warrenton just after the rear guard of Hooker's Grand Division had left. He found large piles of supplies burning and the railroad bridges on the Orange and Alexandria Railroad destroyed. These facts confirmed reports that Burnside was moving his entire army toward Fredericksburg.[16]

Now knowing the intentions of the Federals, General Lee put the remainder of General Longstreet's First Corps in motion toward Fredericksburg on the morning of November 19. Jackson was initially allowed to remain in the Valley but on November 20 he was directed to move to the vicinity of Orange Court House in order to be in a better position to unite with the rest of the army if a battle materialized. Lee felt that leaving Jackson in position to threaten the right flank of the Army of the Potomac was wise. Lee, meanwhile, accompanied the main body of the First Corps and reached Fredericksburg on November 20. His force at that point numbered some 45,000 men. When he first arrived the Union army was massed on Stafford Heights just opposite the town, and batteries were being placed in position; but after two days the concentration began to disperse out of view to the rear. This movement Lee correctly interpreted as a dispersal to more convenient bivouac areas, as well as an attempt to gain cover from any Confederate batteries that he might erect behind the town.[17]

Lee did not plan initially to defend the Rappahannock River barrier, but rather hoped to delay the Federal advance as much as possible and then retire to a line based on the North Anna River. The tactical disadvantages of the ground for the defender and the desire to inflict a decisive defeat on the Union army were his two most important reasons for wishing to fall back to the North Anna before making a serious stand. At Fredericksburg, the terrain on the east bank dominated the plain on which the town stood; if artillery batteries were placed there in sufficient quantities, they could inhibit any counterstroke the defender might attempt.

Lieutenant General Jackson was of the same opinion and right up to the day of the battle argued for a stand at the North Anna. With the delay of the Union advance, however, General Lee was persuaded by logistical and psychological considerations to change his mind and attempt to stop the Union advance immediately. The rich Rappahannock River valley contained large amounts of subsistence and forage which he did not want to surrender without a fight.[18] In addition to this consideration, Lee saw the possibility of delivering a blow to Northern morale by fighting on the Rappahannock. In a letter to President Davis in Richmond on November 25, he reasoned:

> All their movements that I have been able to discover look to a concentration at this point, and it appears to me that should General Burnside change his base of operations, the effect produced in the United States would be almost equivalent to a defeat. I think, therefore, he will persevere in his present course, and the longer we can delay him, and throw him into the winter, the more difficult will be his undertaking. It is for this reason that I have determined to resist him at the outset, and to throw every obstacle in the way of his advance.[19]

This decision to stand at Fredericksburg later proved both Lee and Jackson correct in their predictions of the advantages and disadvantages of the Rappahannock line.

By November 26, increasing signs of an imminent crossing by the Union army caused Lee to recall Jackson to the main army. Thus, the entire Confederate army was massed in a position along the south bank of the Rappahannock by December 5, prepared to resist any attempt by the Federals to cross and move south to Richmond.

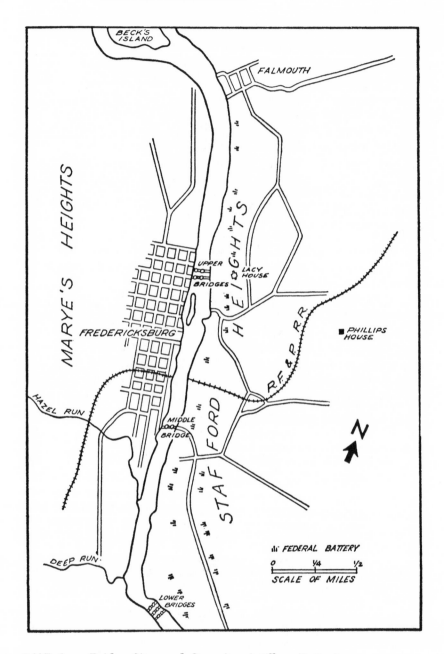

MAP 3 — Bridge Sites and Covering Artillery Batteries
Based on Plate XXV, No. 4, *Atlas to Accompany the Official Records.*

CHAPTER IV

CALM BEFORE THE STORM

By the time the ponderous pontoon wagons began arriving near his headquarters on November 25, General Burnside's hopes for implementing his original campaign plan had disappeared. Five days before, the growing number of Confederate soldiers and batteries gathering on the heights back of the city had given ample evidence of the amassing of Lee's army. Long plumes of black smoke rising in the crisp winter air, from hundreds of Rebel campfires in the woods southeast of Fredericksburg, indicated an additional concentration of troops.

The Union command felt sure that at least Longstreet with most of his corps was in position to dispute the crossing of the Rappahannock; how many more Confederates awaited them could not immediately be determined. Burnside was convinced that since he had not succeeded in slipping past Lee and getting well on the road to Richmond before the Confederate general could move to intercept him, it would be necessary to devise a new plan. If deception would not work, possibly a simple power play implemented by his superiority in numbers might succeed. Now that the enemy was fully alerted to the Union strategy, Burnside decided to plan for a tactical crossing of the river, the success of which would be insured by the greater strength of his forces.[1]

It was no simple matter to transport a large army over an unfordable river in the face of an alert and energetic foe. A miscalculation might lead to disaster if the enemy could attack the forward portion of the army before the main body could be crossed in support. Fully aware of the problems he faced, General Burnside had the engineers survey the river from Fredericksburg south to Port Royal for possible crossing sites. The steep banks of the Rappahannock near Fredericksburg would have to be graded down before troops, especially artillery, could board a pontoon bridge. This grading could be done without too much difficulty on the friendly side of the river, but on the hostile side it would be a serious undertaking.

In the vicinity of Skinker's Neck, some fourteen miles downstream, the terrain was particularly suitable, since at this point it would be possible to transport the army across the river without a fight. Some thought was also given to the possibility of crossing near Port Royal, which was even farther down the river. Here the navy's gunboats could have provided support for a crossing which would have placed the Union army in a position to regain their tactical freedom and move south swiftly without immediate interference from the Rebels.[2]

After careful study, it was decided to cross at Skinker's Neck rather than Port Royal, and engineers made preparations for the crossing. Orders were issued to all the units and planning was well underway when, to everyone's dismay, Union working parties reported the arrival of large Rebel forces on the opposite bank and the erection of batteries to cover possible landing points. The navy at Port Royal also reported increased Confederate activity and, on December 4, after being shelled by new Rebel batteries, the Union gunboats were forced to drop downstream.[3]

Once again prompt countermeasures by Lee had foiled Burnside's attempt to make an unopposed crossing of the Rappahannock. Burnside's solution to this dilemma was a rather unusual one. He decided that the Union army should cross directly into Fredericksburg. Southern forces, he reasoned, were already spread along the river from that city to Port Royal and could detect any attempted crossing. Therefore, by driving directly into Fredericksburg, which undoubtedly was considered by Confederates as the least likely crossing point since no Union preparations had been made, Burnside could achieve what little surprise was possible under the circumstances and could attack with his whole force only a portion of the Confederate army. He decided to span the river at two points. One column would cross directly over into the town and a second column would transit at a point about one and one-half miles below the town.[4]

On November 27, President Lincoln and General Halleck visited the army to confer with Burnside about his plans for continuing the offensive. President Lincoln did not voice any serious objections to a crossing at Fredericksburg; but he proposed that, in addition to the dual crossing, two other columns should cross farther down the Rappahannock and act in cooperation with the main army. Lincoln's plan was not adopted because of the time required to equip and supply these two auxiliary columns.[5] While the President and the General-in-Chief both took great pains to assure Burnside that they were not trying to rush him into a premature assault, he reacted to the pressure of Northern public opinion.

Many military commentators have criticized Burnside for attempting to overwhelm Lee after having given him ample time to prepare his position. The selection of the points of crossing has been scored by these same experts; for example, G. F. R. Henderson, the noted British authority, said:

> Bearing in mind that there was an alternative course open to Burnside, [crossing the Rappahannock north of Falmouth by the fords] and that he was not even bound to advance at all, is there another instance in history where a general, free to act, ran so great a risk with so little justification?[6]

There is justification for the argument that Lee could have been flanked out of his position behind Fredericksburg, as that feat was successfully accomplished by General Hooker the next summer. This could also have been accomplished after the river had been crossed at the designated points. The General's option to delay any further, however, was restricted by the Northern public's demand that he move against Lee before winter set in. This psychological pressure on Burnside was indicated by an admission made by General Sumner in answering a question later posed by the Committee on the Conduct of the War. He said in part:

> I was in favor of crossing the Rappahannock, because I knew that neither our government nor our people would be satisfied to have our army retire from this position, or to go into winter quarters, until we knew the force that was on the other side of the river; and the only way in which we could learn that was by going over there and feeling of them.[7]

Whether Lincoln had specifically ordered him to attack or not, Burnside well understood that McClellan had been removed, at least ostensibly, because he had not come to grips with the enemy fast enough to suit the President, and that he (Burnside) had been appointed to initiate some action before going into winter quarters. But granting the necessity for the Union army to cross the Rappahannock and engage the Confederates, General Burnside could hardly have devised a less imaginative plan. He had based his strategy on the conviction that Lee had detached Jackson to the south at Port Royal and that a quick move on the shortest possible line would enable him to crush Lee before Jackson could arrive in support.

In planning for the crossing in the vicinity of Fredericksburg, Union engineers were able to take advantage of the steep banks of the river for protection from Confederate artillery fire originating from batteries on the slopes behind the town. Unless cannon were stationed directly on the low bluffs at the river's edge, they could not bear on the surface of the river. At the points of crossing the banks rose abruptly from the water to about thirty feet, and direct fire of the guns could not clear them with a sufficiently low trajectory to hit pontoons on the water. Howitzers could fire a high trajectory, but they lacked the range and observation points for accurate fire on targets as small as the pontoon bridges.

Burnside's strategy called for speed. Initially, five bridges were planned to enable the grand divisions, along with supporting artillery, to cross as rapidly as possible. Starting at the town, two bridges were to be thrown across opposite the foot of Hawke Street, the site of an old rope ferry, and a third near the burned-out railroad bridge at the lower end of the town. The first two were known to the Federals as the upper bridges and the third as the middle bridge. About one mile south of the middle bridge, near the mouth of Deep Run, two more bridges were to be built, one of which was to have approaches for artillery. These pontoons were known as the lower bridges. The distance between the upper and lower bridges was almost two miles.

There were two engineer units available for construction of the bridges: a battalion of regulars and a brigade of volunteers. The regulars were assigned to lay the lowest bridge while the volunteer brigade, commanded by Brigadier General Daniel P. Woodbury, was charged with construction of the four others.[8] The plan called for the bridge trains to move to the river at 3 a.m., December 11, so that by daylight, or shortly thereafter, the troops could start across. To cover the engineers during construction work, massive quantities of artillery and infantry support was to be provided, and a regiment of infantry sharpshooters was to further safeguard each bridge.[9]

Brigadier General Henry J. Hunt, chief of artillery for the Army of the Potomac, was made responsible for the ordnance covering the crossing and deployment of the army on the Fredericksburg plain. Because the artillery reserve was depleted by the assignment of batteries to divisions, General Hunt had to withdraw all but one battery from each division in order to provide coverage for the army's crossing. Altogether, he collected 147 guns of all calibres, dividing them into four commands assigned to cover the opposite bank of the river at the bridge sites and the plateau beyond. The Right group, consisting of forty heavy and light guns, was positioned from Falmouth Dam to a ravine just below Falmouth village. This group, under the command of Lieutenant Colonel William Hays, had the mission of clearing enemy troops and guns out of the opposite hills and the slopes running down to the town of Fredericksburg. The Right Center group of thirty-eight guns took position from the ravine south of Falmouth to a point close to the middle bridge site. Colonel Charles T. Tompkins directed this section of the line and was made responsible for covering the three bridges being built opposite Fredericksburg. He was ordered to suppress rifle fire from the buildings on the bank and also sweep the streets leading to the river so that no enemy reinforcements could be brought forward to harrass the engineers. His batteries also were to prevent the Rebels from cannonading the bridges.

The Left Center group, under the command of Colonel Robert O. Tyler, was in position from a point just below the middle bridge to a point opposite Deep Run. His twenty-seven guns were to sweep the open plain between Hazel Run and Deep Run, depriving the enemy of this area for movements of reserves to or from either flank. This would require the Confederates to make all lateral movements over roundabout roads to the rear of their position.

The Left Group of batteries, consisting of forty-two pieces under Captain Gustavus A. DeRussy, extended the line of batteries of the Left Center group southwards to Pollock's Mill. These guns were to cover the lower bridges and also protect the left flank of the army by preventing enemy use of the Massaponax river bridges.[10] Federal artillery was ranged along the high ground of the river bank, and a few heavy guns backed up the line from positions on a second tier of higher ground.

The effectiveness of these Union batteries has been exaggerated in previous accounts. A check of the distance from the Union guns to the main Confederate battle line quickly reveals their actual capabilities. The average range from the Right and Right Center guns to the main Confederate position was 1,100 yards, the Left Center 5,400 yards, and the Left Battery 3,000 yards. These ranges were measured from the battery locations to those parts of the Rebel position directly opposite them. The guns of the Left Center, for example, could mass on a portion of the Confederate left at a range of only 1,500 yards, but to strike home against the main body would have called for an increased range of 3,900 yards. The maximum ranges of the rifled guns of the period were 6,200 yards for the 10-pounder Parrott and 4,000 yards for the 3-inch rifle.[11] These two types constituted more than two-thirds of the Union batteries. While these guns could reach the enemy's main position, accuracy at such a range was difficult. In addition, the poor ammunition checked the gunners' efforts to deliver overhead fire when their infantry was close to the enemy's position.[12] These guns could, however, completely dominate the banks of the river and the level plain extending to the ridgeline beyond. This fact alone was sufficient to discourage any Rebel counterattack. A careful reconnaissance by artillery commanders smoothed the way for moving guns into position under cover of darkness the night before the attempted crossing. This movement into position had to be accomplished quietly to avoid alerting the opposing pickets to the strategy.

General Burnside called a meeting of his grand division commanders at noon on December 9 and issued his orders for the crossing to begin at daylight on December 11. Only general instructions were issued to guide the grand divisions after they had crossed, since the enemy's countermeasures could not be accurately forecast. General Sumner was to initiate action by marching his grand division into Fredericksburg via the upper and middle bridges as soon as they were completed and ensconcing his corps in the city and along the river bank. As soon as General Hooker's Center Grand Division started across the same bridges, Sumner was to move his unit straight to the front and seize the heights over the Plank and Telegraph Roads. This ridgeline, called Marye's Heights, could provide security for the remainder of the army as it crossed the river. General Hooker was to follow close behind Sumner so that his men could support the move to take Marye's Heights. In addition to defending Sumner's right flank, Hooker was to be prepared to support the movements of General Franklin, who was to cross his grand division over the lower bridges as soon as they were completed and move his command south down the Old Richmond Road. His further movements were to be governed by circumstances, until additional orders were received from the Commanding General.[13] This plan of crossing was evidently based on the assumption that the enemy position was lightly held and could easily be carried by a quick assault. The movement of General Franklin down the Old Richmond Road was designed to separate the wings of the Confederate army so that they could be defeated piecemeal.[14]

On the other side of the river, the Confederate command prepared to resist Union attempts to cross the river. General Lee was faced with the problem of protecting a long river line against an enemy equipped to bridge the river simultaneously in several indeterminable places, forcing Confederates into widespread defense. He did not know for certain whether Burnside would cross at all, but the tenor of the Northern papers which he received led him to believe that a crossing was impending and the calendar told him that it must be soon.

Lee's plan for the defense of the river was simple and effective. Unable to be strong everywhere at once, he determined to employ a type of mobile defense covering the most likely crossing sites so that when the attempt was made, he could delay the enemy long enough to concentrate his army for battle. Federal activity at Port Royal and Skinker's Neck indicated the possibility of a crossing to flank his Fredericksburg position. As soon as the Second Corps arrived, General Jackson dispatched Ewell's Division, commanded by Brigadier General Jubal A. Early, to the vicinity of Skinker's Neck to prepare and erect batteries. Major General Daniel H. Hill's Division, reinforced with some of the reserve batteries, was sent on a similar mission to Port Royal. The remainder of Jackson's corps was placed in bivouac in the vicinity of Guinea Station, midway between the wings of the army, ready to rush to either flank when the blow finally fell. This disposition put Lee in a position to retort quickly and with telling force when his opponent finally revealed his intentions.

Lee had all of Longstreet's First Corps in position at Fredericksburg, and these troops were picketing the river bank from Falmouth Dam south to the Massaponax River. Because of the dominating heights on the Union side of the river, Lee entertained no hope of preventing a crossing, but he did intend to delay the enemy as long as possible so that he could assemble his forces before a battle took place. To take advantage of the shelter of the buildings in Fredericksburg, the picket reserve was posted there. Despite bitterly cold weather, the ill-clad Southern outposts waited patiently for the bluecoats.[15]

In the high command of the Union army, all was not as well as it should have been on the eve of the battle. In contrast to the confidence of the Confederates, Union councils were apprehensive. The misgivings of many of the top commanders when Burnside assumed command had now turned to outright distrust. General Hooker was free with criticism, and even junior officers voiced gloomy predictions that the Union army was heading directly into "Lee's trap," as they termed it. General Burnside, whose self-confidence was almost nonexistent anyway, was certainly not reassured by these freely expressed comments, which also were corrosive to the morale of the troops. On Monday, December 8, Burnside called together his chief subordinates, both line and staff, and expressed his disapproval in plain terms. He said in part:

> I have heard your criticisms, gentlemen, and your complaints. You know how reluctantly I assumed the responsibility of command. I was conscious of what I lacked; but still I have been placed where I am and will do my best. I rely on God for wisdom and strength. Your duty is not to throw cold water, but to aid me loyally with your advice and hearty service. . . .[16]

These were strange words from a commanding general on the eve of an important and difficult operation. They disclose, however, the suspicious and insecure climate in which both Burnside and his commanders were trying to operate.

On December 10, the troops were ready for the opening round. According to orders, they had cooked three days' rations and placed them in their haversacks. The battle allowance of sixty rounds of ammunition for each man was distributed, forty rounds in the cartridge box and twenty rounds in the pocket. The weather of the preceding week had been very cold; the temperature dropped below freezing at night, and a light snow lay on the ground. The troops did their best to keep warm, their efforts aided by good timber in the bivouac areas. The morale of the soldiers seems to have been resigned, but not particularly low, considering the attitude of many of the officers.[17] That thoughts turned to home as well as to the impending battle was well illustrated by an incident which occurred on the picket line one afternoon before the battle began. A Union regimental band was standing in a clearing on the side of Stafford Heights playing an impromptu serenade for a group of off-duty soldiers. Some Rebel pickets called across the river and asked the band to play "Yankee Doodle." The Confederates cheered the song when it was played, so the band struck up "Dixie," after which the Yankees cheered. Finally, as the sun went down out of sight, the band struck up the familiar "Home, Sweet Home," and a thoughtful silence fell over the troops on both sides of the river. The bandsmen put away their instruments and quietly went back to their bivouac.[18]

At the camps on both sides of the Rappahannock, veterans settled down to get what rest they could, while many recruits wondered how they would like their first "look at the elephant."[19]

CHAPTER V

VALOR ON THE BRIDGES

Before daybreak on December 11, Union engineer units rolled the bridge trains from the parks to the edge of the river and began construction. With the temperature at 24 degrees, working in the water was slow and uncomfortable, and at the lower bridge site inch-thick ice impeded the operation.[1] Three of the five bridges arrived almost simultaneously at the river edge; however, problems delayed construction of the lower bridges being built by the regulars, who were unable to get the pontoon wagons close to the shore. It was necessary to move all matériel by hand the last two hundred yards. These bridges were not actually begun until 7 a.m., two hours later than the beginning of construction of the upper and middle bridges.[2] General Hunt's artillery batteries moved into position to support the bridge builders, and a regiment of infantry sharpshooters was posted at the starting end of each bridge. It was confidently assumed that the artillerymen and sharpshooters would suppress Confederate pickets attempting to interfere with the workers.[3] While the engineers toiled as quietly as possible, on the other side of the river Confederate pickets were trying to figure out what the Yankees were up to. They suspected the imminence of a Federal crossing because of reports received from Confederate sympathizers living behind enemy lines and because of the accelerated tempo of Union troop movements. On the morning of the tenth, a "good Virginia lady," as Lieutenant Colonel E. P. Alexander of the Confederate artillery termed her, called across the river to a Rebel picket that Union troops had just received rations for three days with orders to cook them immediately.[4]

General Longstreet had given Major General Lafayette McLaws' division responsibility for the defense of the river front. McLaws, in turn, placed Brigadier General William Barksdale with his brigade in position along the river. Barksdale was reinforced during the early morning hours by the Eighth Florida Regiment, a small body of around two hundred men from Brigadier General E. A. Perry's brigade. Barksdale placed his troops from right to left in the following manner: Eighth Florida, Seventeenth Mississippi, a detachment of the Eighth

Florida, and the Eighteenth Mississippi. The Seventeenth Mississippi line began at the rope ferry and extended south to one-half mile above Deep Run, with a third group of the Eighth Florida in position on their left flank. The Eighteenth Mississippi tied in its left flank from the end of the Seventeenth's line to a point one-quarter of a mile south of Deep Run. The two remaining regiments of the brigade, the Thirteenth and Twenty-first Mississippi, were kept in the vicinity of the market house in Fredericksburg as a reserve.[5] The Mississippians were in position to fire down into the river with very little exposure to themselves. They had taken advantage of the substantially built houses along the bluff above the river, using them as sharpshooter posts and reinforcing them with rifle pits and connecting trenches.[6] In some cases, cellars were loopholed and proved to be almost impervious to artillery fire.

That night a foggy mist rose from the river, a mist so thick that the opposite bank was concealed from view. Early in the evening, the unmistakable hum of a large army on the move drifted over to the Confederates, together with the sound of artillery moving into position somewhere along Stafford Heights. By midnight, Barksdale was sure the Federals were about to cross the river, so he doubled his picket line and had all troops awakened and alerted. At 2 a.m., he sent word to General McLaws that the crossing attempt would probably start soon. Longstreet had designated McLaws to be responsible for firing a prearranged signal of two cannon shots to alert the army that the Union crossing was beginning. The noises that were clearly heard throughout the night, although nothing could actually be seen, indicated by 4:30 a.m. that the construction of the bridges had started. Barksdale reported to McLaws that the crossing was underway and that he would fire as soon as his men could see a target. Almost simultaneously, at 5 a.m., the deep sound of the two signal guns and the sharp popping of Barksdale's rifles broke the morning stillness.[7]

The engineers, working as quickly and quietly as possible, pushed the pontoon bridges into the river section by section, until one of the bridges at the Rope Ferry and the one near the railroad bridge extended almost two-thirds of the way across. Swirling fog still obscured the opposite shore and the men working on the forward ends of the bridges, by now less than eighty yards from the west bank, could detect no signs of the enemy. Brigadier General Daniel P. Woodbury anxiously superintended the operation of his brigade which was responsible for the bridges at the city. Without warning, the Mississippi sharpshooters fired a volley into the workmen on the two bridges, killing one captain and wounding two privates.[8] The Confederates kept up a steady fire until all the engineers had been driven off the bridges and taken cover. Federal infantry supports at each bridge opened fire, but the range was too great and visibility too poor for accurate shooting. The Union artillery was able to silence some of the sharpshooters, but the cannon were located too high on the ridge above the river to fire effectively into the houses on the east bank. General Hunt withdrew thirty-six light 12-pounder guns from the divisions and posted twenty-four of them on the river bank behind the upper bridges and twelve on the river bank behind the middle bridge. These guns pounded the shelters of the enemy until Confederate fire ceased altogether. The engineers returned to their work; but before a single plank could be laid, Barksdale's men opened fire again and cleared the workers from the pontoons in short order. Repeated artillery barrages silenced the Confederate sharpshooters temporarily; but, as soon as any attempt was made to begin the work again, they resumed fire.[9]

While this stalemate continued at the Fredericksburg bridges, the lower bridges were being completed. Major James Magruder of the Fifteenth New York Engineers was placing his last section of pontoons in place at 8:15 a.m., when a small group of skirmishers ran to the edge of the bank and fired a volley at his men, wounding six of them. The infantry and artillery batteries supporting Magruder immediately returned the fire of these sharpshooters and dispersed them quickly. At the lower bridges, the guns dominated the west bank because there was no cover for Rebel pickets. To fire on the engineers, they had to stand in full view on the bank and fire down on the pontoons, which completely exposed them to the point-blank fire of Federal guns. Several bold attempts were made to interfere with the construction, but all of them were unsuccessful. Major Magruder's bridge was ready for use by 9 a.m.[10]

The regulars, under Lieutenant Charles E. Cross, were delayed by ice in the river, but by 11 a.m. they had completed the second of the lower bridges, with approaches for all arms. General Burnside, informed of the completion of the lower bridges, ordered General Franklin to hold his position without crossing any troops. Franklin was to employ troops only if the Confederates attempted to destroy his bridges.[11]

At Fredericksburg the bridge-building remained at a standstill because of Confederate opposition. General Woodbury, in an attempt to inspirit his men to stand the sniping and go on with the work, took a group of eighty volunteers from the Eighth Connecticut to complete at least one of the bridges. They rushed down to the water's edge about 10 a.m. But, before any materials could be picked up, several of the men were shot down, and the remainder refused to go on with the work.[12]

The continued failure of the engineers to complete the bridges near the town was ruining the one hope of attacking Lee while his army was still divided. General Burnside ordered a general bombardment of Fredericksburg to begin at 12:30 p.m. in the hope of knocking the Mississippians out of their shelters by a concentrated fire. Every one of the 183 pieces of artillery that would bear on the town was directed to open fire with both shell and solid shot.[13] Thus began what was probably the most concentrated bombardment of such a small target ever to be made in the United States. The fog still hung in the low places and concealed the city from the Union gunners on Stafford Heights; only the spires of City Hall and some of the churches were visible above the mist. The view from the Confederate lines was impressive, with a solid rim of fire marking the line of guns on Stafford Heights, heightened by a continuous roar of exploding shells and tumbling masonry in the town. In the Federal gun positions, much could be heard but little seen of the effect of the fire, except that here and there a column of black smoke rising almost straight into the air would mark the location of a building fired by the bombardment.[14]

The bombardment was maintained until 2:30 in the afternoon when, one by one, the batteries fell silent after firing an average of fifty rounds per gun into the city.[15] Except for the property damage inflicted, this bombardment made little impression on the defenders. They simply took cover with the few remaining civilians in the cellars of the houses and waited out the storm. When the firing ceased, they moved back to their vantage points and repulsed another attempt to complete the bridges.[16]

Time now began to be a problem, since seven hours of precious daylight had slipped by without any improvement in the situation. General Hunt evolved a plan to break the deadlock and sought permission from Burnside to send infantry across the river in the pontoons, which were not yet placed in the bridges, and drive the sharpshooters away from the edge of the river. Burnside gave his permission and left the execution of the plan to Hunt who called for volunteers. He was offered Colonel Norman J. Hall's brigade of Howard's Second

Division, Second Corps, for the work. Men from the Seventh Michigan were to cross at the upper bridge, while the Eighty-ninth New York provided the party to cross at the middle bridge. The artillery was to open fire again for a short time to cover the movement of the volunteers to the boats. The move across the river in the pontoons was to begin when the firing ceased.[17]

At 3 p.m., the first detachment of one hundred volunteers from the Seventh Michigan rushed down to the boats while the artillery kept up its cannonade of the town. A scattered fire from the Confederates routed the engineer crews that were to man the boats, so that a slight delay ensued before it was decided to push on without them. The artillery fire lifted and three pontoons, loaded with seventy men, started across.[18] They were met with a heavy volley from the west bank, but only one man was killed and several wounded while actually in the boats. When the assault troops reached about two-thirds of the way across, they were shielded from the Confederates' fire by the thirty-foot river bank. Forming under the bank, the Seventh Michigan charged up into the town and secured the first street up from the river, Sophia Street.[19]

As soon as the boats could be returned to the east bank, the remainder of the Seventh Michigan was ferried over, as well as the Nineteenth and Twentieth Massachusetts, with orders to extend the tiny bridgehead. The Seventh and Nineteenth regiments held the buildings facing Sophia Street, while the Twentieth Massachusetts was kept in reserve on the river bank to insure control of both ends of the pontoon bridge. Now able to work unmolested, the engineers completed one of the upper bridges by sundown, about 4:30 p.m.

With the bridge complete, the remaining three regiments of Hall's brigade rushed across to support the movement into the city.[20] General Barksdale's men were forced to give up the river bank as soon as the Seventh Michigan made its assault. The Confederate reserves attempted to hold Caroline Street, the second one from the river. Infiltrating Federals made their position untenable, so they fell back to Princess Anne Street and companies of men were stationed to cover each cross street leading up from the river.[21] The Seventh Michigan and Nineteenth Massachusetts were brought to a halt along Caroline Street, and the remaining troops in the brigade were crowded into a small four-block area with the entire Second Division pushing across the bridge to support them. Colonel Hall requested that the remainder of the division remain on the east bank until his men could clear the enemy from the houses to their front. This request was denied. He was ordered instead to push the enemy back immediately and make room for the deployment of fresh troops.

The Twentieth Massachusetts was formed in column on Hawke Street and ordered to pierce the Rebel line on Princess Anne Street. It was rapidly getting darker and the streets did not allow any room for maneuver, so the Twentieth charged straight into the face of the Confederate position. Whole platoons were swept away by the steady volleys of Barksdale's men.[22] In the space of fifty yards, the Twentieth lost almost one hundred men killed and wounded.[23] The Rebel line was broken, however; and Barksdale, on order from General McLaws, began his withdrawal from the city.

At the same time this action was taking place, one hundred men of the Eighty-ninth New York Regiment crossed in four pontoons in the vicinity of the railroad bridge. They quickly captured the buildings that dominated the bridge site, taking sixty-five prisoners including a complete company from the Eighth Florida Regiment. The rest of the New York regiment followed in boats, and together they cleared the enemy from the river front to Caroline Street. Only a desultory fire was kept up between the Rebel skirmishers on Princess Anne Street and the Union pickets on Caroline Street until finally the Confederates withdrew altogether.[24] The engineers went to work on the middle bridge and completed it about 4:30 p.m.

When General Barksdale received the order to withdraw, his fighting spirit was aroused, and he at first refused to obey, hoping to drive the Yankees into the river. With nightfall and the collapse of his line by the railroad bridge, plus the penetration of his Princess Anne Street position by the Twentieth Massachusetts, he reluctantly obeyed the renewed order to withdraw. He commanded the Twenty-first Mississippi to cover the withdrawal and sent runners to each of his detachments to insure that all the troops received the order in time to make good their escape. The withdrawal proceeded smoothly, except for the last detachment in contact. This unit was under the command of Captain Lane Brandon, who discovered that the leading company of the Twentieth Massachusetts was under the command of Henry L. Abbott, his former classmate at Harvard Law School. Brandon decided that he would not be driven back by Abbott and that he would whip him then and there. He turned his men about, proceeded to attack the head of the column, and for a moment drove the Federals back. Barksdale, seeing the danger of this unit being surrounded, peremptorily sent an order to Brandon to retire. Upon his refusal, the general had the young captain placed under arrest, and the next in command conducted the remainder of the withdrawal without incident.[25]

General Burnside was now in a position to move more men across the river, preparatory to making an assault on the divided Confederate army. He ordered General Franklin to send one brigade of infantry across the lower bridges and set up a small bridgehead to protect the pontoons during the night. The Second Brigade of the Third Division, Sixth Corps, under Brigadier General Charles Devens, Jr., was selected for this work. These troops drove off the Confederate pickets who had taken up a position in some farm buildings near the bridges. For the rest of the night a solid line was established with pickets at the front. No serious attempt was made by the Confederates to assault this position. They were content to watch the Union activities from a distance.[26]

Brigadier General Oliver O. Howard with his Second Division of the Second Corps was ordered to clear the enemy from the city limits. Colonel Rush C. Hawkins' brigade of the Ninth Corps crossed the middle bridge, drove the enemy from the area, and sent patrols to connect with Howard's men on the right. The troops in the city were under the command of General Howard who pushed his patrols after the retreating Confederates until the invaders controlled the entire city.[27] During the night, the engineers completed the second of the upper bridges. General Franklin discovered there were enough pontoons left to span the river one more time in his area, so on the morning of December 12 a third bridge was built at the lower bridge site. This sixth bridge was satisfactory only for infantry movement. The remainder of the grand divisions were bivouacked in positions convenient to the crossing points so that they would be ready to cross the river next morning at daylight.[28]

Over in Fredericksburg, some of the troops got out of hand and began to loot the town. Most of the townspeople had fled the city before the battle started. Others had abandoned their homes following the heavy bombardment of the city during the early afternoon, but a few hardy citizens stayed to look after their property. Where a house was still occupied by the owners, nothing was taken; but, if a home was empty, the soldiers assumed that the property it contained had been abandoned. The record of the Second Division is spotty, with some regiments refraining from looting and others engaging in it. In the southern end of the city, held by Hawkins' brigade, street sentries had orders to arrest any Union soldier caught inside a building. The severity of the cold that night made it difficult to enforce such regulations, but Colonel Edgar Kimball of the Ninth New York asserted that at least in his sector the order was "literally obeyed."[29] A great deal of the property taken from the homes was left in the streets or simply smashed or defaced because it could not be carried off. The soldiers, however, were not the only guilty parties for during the height of the looting, citizens of the town were seen slipping into their neighbors' homes looking for items of value.[30]

The sacking of Fredericksburg continued for the entire period of the Federal occupation, with only sporadic efforts of the Union commanders to control it. The picture was not all black, however, as some of the troops did what they could to save property. The heavy bombardment of the city had started several fires. The men of the 106th Pennsylvania Regiment were all members of volunteer fire companies in Philadelphia, and they set to work to put out the conflagrations. After a long struggle, the fires were brought under control and the volunteer firemen went back to soldiering.[31]

Nightfall of December 11 found General Burnside's initial plan thwarted by the spirited defense of the river bank by Barksdale and his Mississippi regiments. Once again, a plan that depended on speed of execution was hobbled at the very start. The fighting of the day served to alert Lee to the probability of an attempt to smash his army in its position behind Fredericksburg. Thus warned, the Confederates were able to recall all detachments downriver to the main army before this attack could be launched. As General Longstreet put it:

> Brigadier General Barksdale with his brigade held the enemy's entire army at the river bank for sixteen hours, giving us abundance of time to complete our arrangements for battle. A more gallant and worthy service is rarely accomplished by so small a force.[32]

The grand division commanders expected to cross their troops that night so that shortly after dawn the attack to take the heights could begin. Inexplicably, Burnside did not take this course. The crossing of the army was not made until morning, putting the Federal plan a full twenty-four hours behind schedule. At daybreak on December 12, the Federal troops started across the Rappahannock.[33] General Franklin sent the Sixth Corps over the lower bridges first to form the right of the grand division line. Major General William F. Smith placed the First Division, commanded by Brigadier General William T. H. Brooks, on the Old Richmond Road with its right flank resting on Deep Run and connecting with the left of Sumner's Grand Division. The Second Division, under Brigadier General Albion P. Howe, extended Brooks's line to the left along the Old Richmond Road. The Third Division, commanded by Brigadier General John Newton, was placed in reserve behind the position of General Howe. The cavalry brigade, led by Brigadier General George D. Bayard, crossed next and was sent forward on reconnaissance. Upon returning from this reconnaissance, the cavalry was placed in reserve near the bridges. Major General John F. Reynolds crossed with his First Corps, the last major element of the Left Grand Division. The Second Division of Brigadier General John Gibbon was placed with his right connecting with General Howe's left and his left pulled back from the Old Richmond Road toward the river. The Third Division, Major General George G. Meade commanding, connected with Gibbon on the right and, running almost at right angles with the Old Richmond Road, rested its left on the river bank at the Smithfield Ravine. Brigadier General Abner Doubleday's First Division was placed in reserve behind the line formed by the Second and Third Divisions.[34] The artillery for each division was returned to division control as the units crossed the bridges. In addition, five batteries of Captain DeRussy's concentration were attached to Franklin's force, giving him at this time a total of eighty-six field guns.[35] The troops finished crossing the bridges and were moving to their assigned places in the line by 1 p.m.

The Right Grand Division was also crossing during the same period and was massing in position in the city. General Howard's Division of the Second Corps, which had crossed the night before, moved over to occupy only the right half of the city. The Third Division, under Brigadier General William H. French, occupied the center portion of the city, while the First Division of Brigadier General Winfield S. Hancock moved into position directly behind French. The remainder of the Ninth Corps crossed on the middle bridge and occupied the left portion of the city, extending beyond to connect with General Franklin's right. The actual movement of troops across Hazel Run to Deep Run was not made until the morning of the thirteenth.[36] In addition to these troop units, General Sumner was also supported by ten batteries of fifty-six guns which crossed with the various divisions of his grand division.[37]

General Hooker's Center Grand Division remained on the east bank of the river, prepared to move to the assistance of either of the other grand divisions. In fact, there was no room in Fredericksburg for additional troops, and adding more men to Sumner's lines would only have increased the confusion. General Burnside now had the major portion of his army in Fredericksburg, and everything was ready for the swift push up to the heights to knock the divided Lee out of his position. But the delay in bringing Lee to battle had invalidated Burnside's initial battle plan; therefore, he had to devise a new one.

General Lee had begun his countermeasures almost at the same moment that he heard McLaws' signal guns. General Jackson was ordered to bring into line the two divisions that were bivouacked near Guinea Station. Major General Ambrose P. Hill's division marched up from its encampment near Yerby and took over a portion of the front line. Jackson's division, commanded by Brigadier General William B. Taliaferro, was placed in reserve behind General Hill. General Jackson's remaining two divisions, under Generals Jubal Early and D. H. Hill, were left watching the lower crossings of the Rappahannock. Lee was afraid that Burnside was only making a feint at Fredericksburg to cover a crossing farther down the river. Even when Confederate observers glimpsed through the fog long columns of Union soldiers crossing the bridges on the morning of December 12, Lee was not convinced that this was the real attack. At noon, he and Jackson made a dangerous personal reconnaissance of General Franklin's position in order to determine the strength of the force which had crossed. Their observations convinced Lee that Burnside was not trying to trick him, and that the crossing was genuine. Only then did he issue the order to Jackson to bring up D. H. Hill and Early to complete the concentration of the army. These troops had a long night march but arrived in time for the battle.[38]

CHAPTER VI

THE BATTLEFIELD

The topography of the Fredericksburg battlefield is particularly well suited to a defensive stand. In order to clarify the remainder of the text, it is necessary to describe the major terrain features which were of importance during the battle.

At Fredericksburg, the Rappahannock River flows almost due south, cutting the operational area into two parts. On the east bank, the town of Falmouth stands at the head of navigation of the river with Falmouth Dam one mile north. The major terrain feature along the east bank is Stafford Heights. This steep ridgeline extends from Falmouth Dam in the north to Pollock's Mill some five miles to the south. Stafford Heights dominates the west bank, as well as the plain beyond, because it rises almost straight up from the river bank. To the east of this high ground, the elevation continues to rise as you leave the river. At the time of the battle, the crest of Stafford Heights was open, the forest starting farther back in the hills. At several points, the ridge was cut by steep wooded ravines formed by the flow of small streams running down to the river.

On the west bank, one-half mile south of Falmouth, the town of Fredericksburg stands on an open plain. A range of hills starting near Falmouth Dam extends in a curve to a point near the Massaponax River, a distance of over six miles. The plain that is formed by these hills and the river varies in width from three-fourths of a mile at Fredericksburg to two and one-half miles in the Lansdown Valley. The plain is cultivated and generally flat but is intersected at right angles by two streams that form obstacles to lateral movement. Hazel Run flows into the Rappahannock just south of Fredericksburg; and Deep Run, which flows through the Lansdown Valley, finally empties into the Rappahannock one-half mile south of Hazel Run. The Massaponax River flows east and passes just south of Prospect Hill, the last feature in the range of hills known as Spotsylvania Heights, and thence into the Rappahannock.

It is apparent then that Fredericksburg stands on a plain bounded

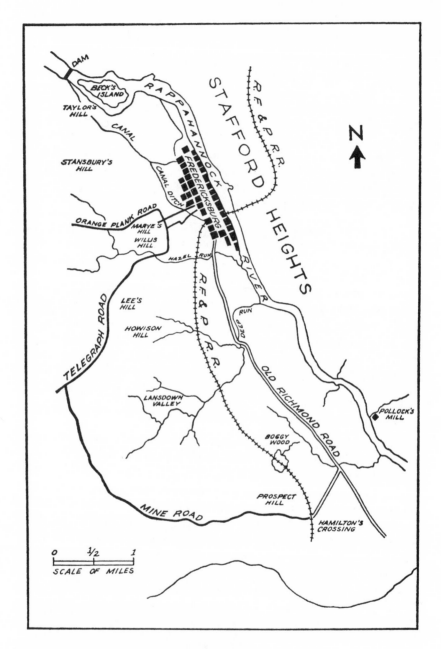

MAP 4 — Fredericksburg Battle Area
Based on sketch map, Freeman, *Lee's Lieutenants*, II, 331.

on the east by the Rappahannock, on the north and west by a series of low hills, and on the south by the Massaponax River. This entire series of features forms a terrain cross-compartment which bars movement west from the river. The major hill masses in the western range are as follows, starting in the north at Falmouth Dam: Taylor's Hill, Stansbury's Hill, Marye's Heights, Lee's Hill, Howison Hill, and Prospect Hill at the end of the range. A second and higher mass of high ground stands behind the first, extending westward. The southern half of this high ground was heavily wooded while the northern half was generally clear.

A number of man-made features assumed considerable importance during the battle. The Richmond, Fredericksburg, and Potomac Railroad crossed the Rappahannock into Fredericksburg at the southern end of the town and, after leaving the city limits, curved south along the river. The tracks, after paralleling the river for about three miles, turned past Prospect Hill at Hamilton's Crossing. The Old Richmond Road ran south from Fredericksburg parallel with the river about half-way between the railroad and the river bank.[1] This road had high earth banks on each side, making a fine temporary breastwork in the open plain.

The town of Fredericksburg extended along the river for slightly more than one mile and was built back from the river an average of five city blocks. This quiet colonial town consisted mostly of substantially built brick and stone buildings and contained a population of over five thousand inhabitants. Two roads connected Fredericksburg with towns to the west. The Orange Plank Road was an extension of William Street, passing west from the town and then up Marye's Heights and on to the Orange Court House.[2] Telegraph Road, an extension of Hanover Street, passed west from the town and then turned south to run along the foot of Marye's Heights. At the end of the heights, Telegraph Road turned east again and passed through the break in the ridge caused by Hazel Run. This road was worn to a level below the plain and was bordered by stone retaining walls.

Fredericksburg contained a series of water mills, and water for their operation was supplied by a canal which ran from Falmouth Dam to a basin on the northern edge of the city. Near the point at which the canal turned east into the city, a paper mill was located, and a millrace branched off from the canal. This millrace flowed in a southerly direction between the outskirts of the city and the hills to the west, finally turning east into the city at its southern edge near the R. F. & P. Railroad depot. The millrace was crossed by bridges at each of the main streets leading from the city, but it was possible to cross it by ford only in a few places. The last feature of importance was an unfinished railroad grade, running southeast from the railroad depot on Prussia Street, past the end of Marye's Heights, and then along the trace of Hazel Run into the hills.

These were the terrain features that General Lee had to defend and General Burnside to seize before any further movement toward Richmond could take place. Lee, the engineer, might be expected to get the maximum military value from any such piece of terrain. His opponent had yet to show his talents in this field.[3]

CHAPTER VII

BLUEPRINT FOR VICTORY–
OR DISASTER

On the afternoon of December 12, General Burnside rode along his lines in the plain about Fredericksburg, scouting the Confederate positions in order to determine his next move. The heavily wooded hills to his front concealed most of the Rebel positions. Only opposite the Union right along Marye's Heights and northward could a few batteries actually be seen. Nevertheless Burnside could readily perceive that his army stood on an open plain, while his enemy occupied all the high ground which dominated that plain. He visited the corps commanders and discussed with them the possible courses of action.[1]

Just as the sun was going down, he stopped at General Franklin's headquarters for a conference. Franklin urged Burnside to order him to mount a strong attack against the heights which formed the Confederate right. He pointed out that time would be required to position the troops for an attack and he hoped the orders would be given in time for a dawn assault. Without committing himself to any particular strategy, Burnside left Franklin with the assurance that orders would be sent to him in two or three hours. As Burnside left the headquarters, Franklin voiced the hope that Burnside's orders would be sent to him by midnight at the latest.[2]

The Commanding General did not return to his headquarters in the Phillips House, high on Stafford Heights, until after midnight. The remainder of the night was spent in maturing a plan of attack and preparing the orders. Burnside was aware that the delay in constructing the bridges had altered the situation on which the original plan had been founded and that a new set of factors had to be considered.[3]

General Burnside had only three possible choices of action. One move would be an attempt to flank the Confederates out of their position by marching downriver, past Prospect Hill on the Old Richmond Road, and around their right flank. Another possibility was to withdraw his troops across the Rappahannock, thus admitting the failure of his campaign, and go into winter quarters. The last of the three

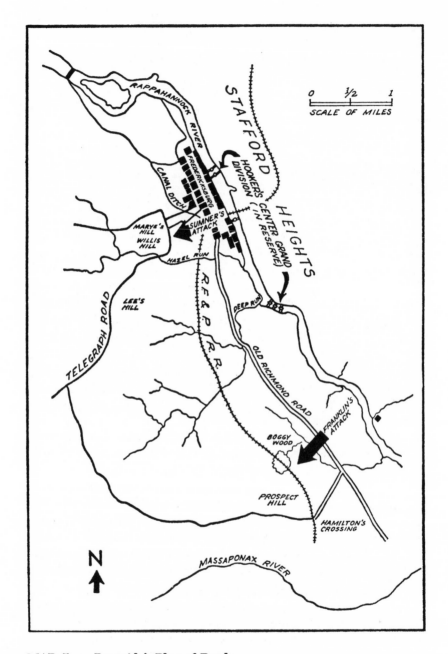

MAP 5 — Burnside's Plan of Battle

Based on sketch map, Freeman, *Lee's Lieutenants*, II, 331.

choices was a frontal assault on the Rebel lines in an attempt to crack Lee's army by a direct power push.

The reasoning which compelled him to cross the river in the first place, long after it was evident that his attempt to side-step Lee had failed, was still operative and precluded any retreat without a battle. In fact, now that his men were in the presence of the enemy, any such move became unthinkable in terms of maintaining morale. The chances of flanking the Rebels out of their strong position were actually slim because, in order to get around the Confederate right flank, the army would have to pass the guns on Prospect Hill which were in a position to enfilade them as they moved downriver. The pontoon bridges could be moved farther to the south, but this would impose further delay in addition to a major readjustment of troop units back across the river. The probable effect of this course was indicated by General Jubal A. Early, one of the division commanders on the Confederate right flank, who wrote:

> Had Burnside moved down the river to the Massaponax, after crossing, or had thrown other bridges across at or near the mouth of that stream, and crossed one of his grand divisions there, he would inevitably have forced us to abandon our line of defense, and fight him on other ground.[4]

This plan could have been more effectively carried out during the initial crossing of the river, but the position in which the army was now situated made this action infeasible.[5]

If it were necessary to attack at all, this frontal assault was the only practical course open to Burnside. Some commentators, such as Trevor N. Dupuy, the contemporary American military historian, have indicated that the Federal commander assaulted the Southern lines when it was entirely unneccessary.[6] This opinion does not take into consideration the effect that a withdrawal would have had, with the troops already in physical contact. Both to the army and to the civilian population of the North, a withdrawal would have been the same as a defeat. Burnside had to attack, and of the possibilities open to him in his present position, a direct assault was his only course.

Fredericksburg was, in effect, a tremendous trap into which Burnside had blundered, one which Lee had prepared with only the faintest hope that his enemy would enter. Until the last minute, Lee could not believe that the Federals would be foolish enough to try a head-on power play. Once Burnside had crossed the river and deployed his army on the open plain, he lost most of the freedom of movement and choice of maneuver that usually resides with the attacker. A private soldier put Burnside's position in simpler but more expressive language when he said just prior to the crossing on December 11, "They want us to get in. Getting out won't be quite so smart and easy. You'll see if it will."[7]

Once the decision for a frontal assault was made, the next question was where the blow should fall. Only on the Federal left was there room to deploy large masses of men and artillery before coming under the point-blank fire of the emplaced Rebel guns. Also, on the left the terrain was most favorable for a Union attack. If Prospect Hill could be seized, the entire Confederate position could be flanked, and Lee would in addition be forced away from his rail link with Richmond. The hills on the right flank of this position were lower and easier to assault than other positions along the line. In the center through the Lansdown Valley, the course of Deep Run made a break in the hill mass and offered a flat pathway for a rapid penetration and break-through of the main Confederate line. This would present one big disadvantage, however, since Rebel positions flanked this approach on both the right and left, placing any attacking column moving up Deep Run under fire from both sides. At Fredericksburg, the Confederate line on Marye's Heights was very close to the Union outposts on the edge of the city, but the restriction of movement and deployment in the city made this position difficult to attack. The presence of the canal in front of the Confederate left, as well as a marshy area, precluded any serious attempt against this flank.[8]

One other feature of the Confederate defenses played an important part in Burnside's planning. In order to facilitate the rapid movement of reinforcements from one part of the defense line to another, the Confederates had constructed a military road running just behind their front line positions and connecting with Telegraph Road near the right flank of Longstreet's Corps. The Union command had learned of the existence of this road from a Negro line-crosser whose home was in the vicinity. General Burnside, faced with severe terrain problems as well as Lee's defensive measures, decided to base his plan of attack on the seizure of this military road.

The plan was simply for Franklin to seize Prospect Hill and thus get control of one end of the military road. He was to keep his command ready for a rapid move down the Old Richmond Road so that, when the heights were taken, his troops could move along the military road behind the crest of the hills. By so doing, the Confederates would be forced out of their entrenchments and taken in flank. This move, if successful, would have the added advantage of forcing the Rebels into difficult country, away from their closest rail communications with Richmond. The second part of this plan envisaged an assault by Sumner, supported by Hooker, against Marye's Heights after Franklin's attack had reached the military road. Such a move by the Federal right was indicated to keep the Confederates pinned down so they could not reinforce their threatened right flank and also prevent them from withdrawing any of their emplaced guns if a retreat should be attempted. The two movements were not to be simultaneous, for Sumner's move was not to be made until Franklin's attack had been successful. It can be seen, therefore, that the attack against the Rebel left was intended to take place only when a beaten enemy was in the process of trying to disengage his forces and was not able to defend the naturally powerful line of defenses.[9] General Burnside later described this basic plan to the Committee on the Conduct of the War in the following manner:

> I wanted to obtain possession of that new road, and that was my reason for making an attack on the extreme left. I did not intend to make the attack on the right until that position had been taken; which I supposed would stagger the enemy, cutting their line in two; and then I proposed to make a direct attack on their front, and drive them out of their works.[10]

This was the plan of the Commanding General, but it had to be communicated in the form of orders to his chief subordinates for execution. The orders were not completed until the morning of December 13, with the grand division commanders receiving them by courier around 7:30 a.m. General Franklin was surprised at the contents of his orders and consulted with his corps commanders before deciding how to carry them out. Specifically, he was directed to hold his command in position for a rapid movement down the Old Richmond Road while he sent at least one division to seize the heights at Hamilton's Crossing.[11] In addition, two divisions of Hooker's Grand Division were placed in support by the bridges on the east bank of the river, to be called on if needed.

General Sumner was ordered to send one or more divisions to seize Marye's Heights to the west of Fredericksburg. He was also directed to extend his left flank units across Hazel Run to link up with Franklin's right flank along Deep Run. The move to assault

Marye's Heights was to be made on the order of the Commanding General. General Hooker was placed in reserve with orders to keep the Fifth Corps and the Third Division of the Third Corps in position to cross the bridges at the city to support General Sumner's attack. The remainder of the Third Corps was to be stationed at the lower bridges, ready to assist the progress of General Franklin's attack.[12]

It can be seen from the orders which Burnside issued to his commanders that he intended to create an open flank in the Rebel position by seizing the high ground which anchored the Confederate right flank. Once this opening was made, the remainder of Franklin's Grand Division could be pushed into the gap to exploit the initial gains. The order to Franklin inferred that additional orders would be sent for the employment of the remainder of the grand division which was being held ready for a swift movement down the Old Richmond Road. Sumner, on the other hand, was to wait for further orders before beginning his attack on the Confederate left, which indicated that his attack was not the main effort. With this issuance of orders, General Burnside set the Army of the Potomac in motion for what he hoped would be a decisive victory.

Coincident with the tactical preparations for the battle, logistical and technical units were busy making their preparations for the support of the army. The Signal Corps had established a network of signal stations which connected the various headquarters with the major subordinate units across the river. Stations were maintained at Phillips House, General Burnside's Headquarters; the Lacy House, General Sumner's Headquarters; and General Franklin's Headquarters on the left flank. Additional stations were set up at vantage points to relay messages and also to observe enemy activities. Signal flags were used to communicate between the stations, precluding operation during hours of darkness or poor visibility. A signal telegraph train, attached to the army, was used for the first time on a tactical battlefield. The telegraph had been used during the Peninsula Campaign, but only in the rear areas. Under the supervision of Captain Frederick Beardslee, telegraphic communications were maintained between Burnside, Sumner, and Franklin. The line to General Franklin was extended across the river after the Left Grand Division had crossed. It stayed in operation until the end of the battle. A line was also laid into Fredericksburg but was not operated because of a shortage of instruments and the effectiveness of the signal flag stations. Extremely poor visibility due to fog and smoke reduced the effectiveness of the more distant flag stations during the Fredericksburg operation. However, those in the city were close enough to maintain contact most of the time. By supplementing these means of communication with mounted couriers, General Burnside had the capability of influencing quickly the action of even his most distant subordinates, a unique opportunity for the commander of such a large army.[13]

Behind the Headquarters buildings at Phillips House, Professor T.S.C. Lowe, the aeronaut, prepared his balloon for flight on the morning of December 13. The "one-man air force" of the Union army had been grounded until this time in order to preserve the secrecy of the river crossing, but he was now allowed to take to the air. His point of ascension would place him directly over Burnside's Headquarters so that any observations made could quickly be communicated to the Commanding General. Arrangements were completed for the use of staff officers as special observers if conditions so warranted. The heavily wooded location of the Confederate position restricted the effectiveness of Lowe's balloon observations, but the device proved valuable in supplying information of friendly troop movements as they took place.[14]

As the troops crossed the river on Friday, the medical officers completed their arrangements for the care of the wounded. Each division selected a spot for its hospital in a covered area to the rear of the unit position. On the Union right, buildings were commandeered for hospital use. Churches and other public buildings were preferred because of their size. On the left, where the ground was more open, most of the unit hospitals were located in ravines near the river in order to secure protection from the direct fire of the Confederate guns on the hills. The ambulance corps was situated along the rear of the Federal line in position to transport the wounded to the nearest hospital. On the east bank of the river, large tent hospitals were erected for the care of the more seriously wounded who might be evacuated from the unit hospitals. Arrangements were made for the transportation of such casualties from these hospitals by train to Aquia Creek landing and then by steamer to Washington. By the evening of December 12, the Medical Department had completed all arrangements for the transportation and care of the wounded.[15]

The logistical support for the army was sufficient to supply the needs of the troops during the coming battle and also during a possible move toward Richmond. Sufficient rations for three days were issued to the men when they crossed the river, and additional food was issued after the crossing. Ordnance trains kept the units supplied with small arms and artillery ammunition. The main supply trains were parked in covered positions on the east bank of the river, ready to cross and accompany the army in its continued movement toward the Rebel capital. General Haupt had made preparations to begin rebuilding the burned railroad bridge over the Rappahannock River. He planned to have trains running into Fredericksburg in plenty of time to support the forward movement of the army. The supply bases at Aquia Creek and Belle Plain were ready to handle the required tonnage to support the army in a campaign of movement.[16]

CHAPTER VIII

FRANKLIN BEGINS THE ASSAULT

Early on the morning of December 13, the last two divisions of Jackson's Second Corps arrived on the battlefield and were placed in position. Jackson was responsible for the southern portion of the Confederate line from Deep Run to Hamilton's Crossing. That part of the line was the most vulnerable to Union attack both because of the low elevation of the ridge and the ample space available in front of it for the deployment of attacking columns. Already, on the morning of December 12, A. P. Hill's Division had moved into the front line to relieve elements of Longstreet's First Corps which moved further to the left to add strength to the Rebel line there. Brigadier General William Taliaferro, commanding Jackson's Division, was placed in reserve behind A. P. Hill. The newly arrived divisions of D. H. Hill and Jubal Early were also placed in reserve behind A. P. Hill, providing Jackson with a very strong reserve force. This situation was unique since, for once, the defending Confederate commander could maneuver sufficient reserve forces to block any penetration of his position.

General A. P. Hill placed four brigades in his front line. Two regiments of Colonel J. M. Brockenbrough's Brigade were placed in position from Hamilton's Crossing north along the R. F. and P. Railroad track which at that point passed just in front of Prospect Hill. Brigadier General J. J. Archer's Brigade was next in line with his right flank connecting with Brockenbrough's left and his left flank resting on a boggy wood that extended east beyond the railroad track. This small wood created a gap of about 600 yards in the Confederate front line but was considered to be impassable. Brigadier General James H. Lane's Brigade rested its right flank 250 yards to the left of the small woods and its left flank on a dirt road which crossed the railroad track at right angles. Brigadier General William D. Pender's Brigade continued the line to the left in the vicinity of Deep Run. The railroad track was used for a picket line with the main position of the troops being from 250 to 450 yards to the rear. The gap between Archer and Lane, caused by the small wood, was covered by Brigadier General Maxcy Gregg's Brigade which was in position to the rear of

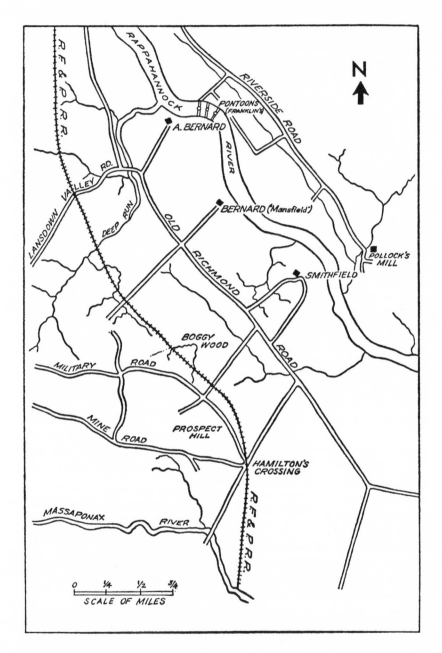

MAP 6 — Prospect Hill and Vicinity
Based on map, Stackpole, *The Fredericksburg Campaign*, p. 189.

the gap along the military road. Brigadier General Edward L. Thomas' Brigade was placed behind the slight gap between Pender and Lane to strengthen that portion of the front line. The remaining two regiments of Brockenbrough's Brigade were placed on Prospect Hill to support the grand artillery battery in position there.

The second line was composed of General Early, commanding Ewell's Division, on the right, and General Taliaferro's Division on the left. Further to the rear, General D. H. Hill's Division formed the reserve. This division was massed behind the right flank of Jackson's position to provide flank protection in case the Federals tried to sweep around Prospect Hill.[1]

The wooded terrain of Jackson's position restricted the employment of artillery, but three batteries were erected. Lieutenant Colonel R. L. Walker was in command of a grand battery of fourteen guns located on Prospect Hill. This high ground was the last terrain feature of importance on the Confederate line. Walker's guns were in a position to deliver effective fire against any troop movements toward Prospect Hill or the Second Corps line to the north. A nine-gun battery was emplaced between Lane's and Pender's positions and another twelve-gun battery was posted across the railroad track in front of Lane's left flank in advance of the main line. This last battery, supported by a regiment of infantry, was intended to deliver flanking fire against troops moving toward Prospect Hill.[2] The open ground between Prospect Hill and the Massaponax River to the south was protected by the cavalry division of Major General J. E. B. Stuart. The horse artillery of this division was placed so that it could cross fire with the batteries on the main line. Stuart's position would flank the entire left side of the Union army as it moved toward the high ground from the river.

The strength of the Confederate line lay in its position rather than in any breastworks constructed by the defending troops. On the day of the battle, only a few of the artillery gun pits were completed. In some places, infantry shelters were not yet finished. The cold weather had frozen the ground and made any engineering work a long slow process. A shortage of tools delayed the construction of field works; therefore, despite the long time Lee had to prepare them, his defenses were not very formidable. At this time, neither side appreciated fully the defensive advantages of field entrenchments, but the coming battle was to impress both armies with their importance.[3]

General Jackson had at his position almost 34,000 infantry and artillery troops. If the cavalry protecting the right flank is included, the total was 42,000.[4] Of the infantry troops, however, only 12,000 were placed on the front line to receive the first shock of the Federal assault. This distribution of strength left ample reserves for use in a counterblow as well as exposing a minimum number of troops to the ravages of the superior Union artillery. With his troops thus alerted and ready for action, Jackson took up his station on Prospect Hill and calmly waited for the Federal attack to begin.

Down on the plain, shrouded by a thick mist rising from the river, General Franklin prepared to execute Burnside's order to attack. Brigadier General James A. Hardie of Burnside's staff reported to Franklin's headquarters as an official observer and to assist the grand division commander in any way possible. Franklin discussed the order with his corps commanders and came to the conclusion that the movement against the heights near Hamilton's Crossing was intended as a kind of reconnaissance-in-force. The twice-repeated injunction to keep his whole command prepared for a rapid movement down the Old Richmond Road seemed to require him to make the initial assault with only a small portion of his force. Major General John F. Reynolds' Corps was designated to make the attack, and he, in turn, entrusted the assault mission to Major General George G. Meade and his Third Division. Meade was to be supported on the right by Gibbon's Division and covered on the left by Doubleday's Division.[5] Franklin approved this employment and felt that, in sending three divisions to make the attack, he was complying with the spirit of Burnside's order.

It was 8:30 a.m. before Meade could get his troops underway. He moved his command across the Smithfield ravine and then downstream about 700 yards before turning the troops at right angles to the river and heading for the high ground. When the troops arrived at the Old Richmond Road, they were forced to halt while the banks on each side of the road were breached to make a passage for the artillery. While this work was being completed, the troops waited patiently in the thick mud of the thawed fields and peered through the dense fog toward the Rebel positions. The weather had moderated on the eleventh but, until the sun dissipated the fog, the damp coldness set the soldiers to stamping their feet and moving about. The Federal skirmishers meanwhile moved out in front of the formation, and the steady gunfire along their line indicated that the Rebel outposts were slowly falling back. Meade formed his attack with the

First and Second Brigades in column, separated by a 300-yard interval, and the Third Brigade deployed to the left to provide flank security.[6] Skirmishers preceded the column, both front and flanks, to avoid surprise in the poor light. This formation had just been completed when two Rebel guns suddenly opened fire on the column from the left rear.

Major John Pelham of Stuart's horse artillery had secured permission to take two of his guns in advance of the Confederate line to harrass the Federal advance. He selected a position near the intersection of the road from Hamilton's Crossing and the Old Richmond Road. Taking advantage of the uneven terrain and protected by a small group of dismounted sharpshooters, he opened fire with solid shot on the close-ranked Federals. His fire was especially damaging because each shot enfiladed the entire formation. Meade, fearing this artillery fire was preparatory to an infantry attack, deployed his Third Brigade in line of battle to the left so that the First and Third formed two sides of a square. The divisional batteries immediately returned the fire of the Rebel guns. General Doubleday's batteries to the left rear also went into action against Pelham. Under the concentrated fire of these batteries, one of the Confederate guns was disabled and forced to withdraw to the rear, but the other gun continued to concentrate its fire on Meade's infantry formation. As soon as the Federal artillery found the range of this gun, it was moved a short distance, only to open fire once more from its new position. After a duel lasting thirty minutes, the Federals finally gained the upper hand and the lone Confederate gun was withdrawn.[7] The sharpshooters protecting this Rebel piece worked their way forward along the Old Richmond Road toward the position held by Meade's skirmishers. However, they were forced back by two companies of the Third Brigade before they could accomplish very much.

When the enemy battery opened fire on Meade, Doubleday was ordered to change front and move down toward the Massaponax River to clear the enemy from this flank of the army and, in addition, to protect the left flank of the First Corps during its attack. Pushing the enemy's sharpshooters back rapidly for about half a mile, Doubleday's men seized a small woods on the bank of the Rappahannock which had been used by the Rebels as a strong point. Having arrived at a position well below the end of the enemy-occupied ridge, Doubleday swung three brigades to face the high ground and moved forward to the Old Richmond Road. His Fourth Brigade was placed on the left flank of his division with the brigade's right flank on the Old Richmond

Road and its left flank on the river. The divisional batteries were placed between the brigade intervals to suppress the fire of the Rebel guns on the high ground.[8] This movement by Doubleday led Jackson to fear an attempt to turn his right flank; therefore, he moved General D. H. Hill's division to support Stuart's dismounted troopers on the threatened flank. When no further movement was made by Doubleday, these troops were recalled and placed in their original reserve position.[9]

General Gibbon, whose division was in place along the Old Richmond Road next to the position held by Smith's Sixth Corps, prepared to move to cover Meade's right flank. At 9 a.m., this division moved directly across the Old Richmond Road and, after reaching halfway between the road and the enemy position, the Third Brigade was halted at the crest of a small rise which afforded some protection from fire coming from the main Rebel positions. The Second Brigade was moved up within supporting distance of the Third, while the First Brigade was placed to the left rear of the Second to support the divisional battery. This movement was made under the cover of the fog. When the troops were in position, they were instructed to lie down and take cover.[10]

At this time, the Federal situation was as follows: Meade had moved opposite the point he was to assault and had begun to make his deployment preparatory to the attack, while Doubleday, on his left, had taken up a position to protect the open flank. Gibbon was on a line slightly ahead of Meade and on his right flank, ready to conform to his forward movement. The skirmish line was engaged along the entire front, while the Rebel batteries remained silent to avoid giving away their positions before the infantry attack began. The thick fog began to lift at 10 a.m. so that the Confederate army could see its adversary clearly for the first time. The martial sight presented by the long blue lines of the thousands of Union soldiers of the Left Grand Division made a deep impression on the watching Confederates. The amphitheatre-like position of the Confederates and the open plain upon which the Federals were deployed enhanced the psychological effect of this sight. The steady ranks of the Unionists, with the line here and there broken by the bright splashes of color in their flags and the sun glinting from the polished arms and cannon, made even Jackson's veterans gasp. Major Heros Von Borcke, a staff officer with Stuart, was so awed that he voiced an uneasiness about the Confederate ability to stop the Yankee assault. General Jackson, his voice showing the peculiar exhilaration he seemed to feel on the eve of a battle, replied confidently, "Major, my men have sometimes failed to *take* a position, but to *defend* one, never!"[11] Despite such confidence, Jackson was soon to feel his position badly shaken by Meade's veterans.

Down on the plain, the Union officers, even with the improvement in the visibility, still were unable to determine much about the Rebel defenses. On the extreme end of the ridge, what looked like a large battery of artillery could be seen, but the enemy's infantry was invisible in the thick woods covering most of their position.

After silencing the two guns which had harrassed his early movement, Meade continued his preparations for the assault. By order of his corps commander, Major General Reynolds, the Third Brigade was placed in line of battle, extending the line of the First Brigade to the left.[12] This placed the left flank of the Third Brigade opposite the end of Prospect Hill, almost to Hamilton's Crossing. The Second Brigade was still in support of the First, about 300 yards to the rear. While this deployment was underway, the divisional batteries of both Meade and Doubleday opened fire on the Confederate battery on Prospect Hill. Although a storm of fire raked the enemy position, not one round was returned in answer. The Rebel gunners had received strict orders not to fire until the Federal infantry came into range.

While the bombardment was in progress, Reynolds joined Meade and indicated again the objective of the attack. Meade was directed to move straight into the nearest point of woods opposite his division and then to take the crest of the hill behind it. Once in control of the crest, the First Brigade was to wheel to the left and take the enemy battery on Prospect Hill from the flank. The Second Brigade was to move up and hold the crest, which the First had seized, while the Third Brigade was to assist in the seizure of Prospect Hill by a movement across the open fields and then up the face of the hill. The point of woods that was indicated as the initial objective was the same boggy woods which covered the gap between Lane and Archer in the Rebel front lines.[13] After a bombardment which lasted over thirty minutes, during which the only sign of enemy occupation of Prospect Hill was indicated by the explosion of two ammunition caissons, the Union batteries ceased fire. With the apparent silencing of any Rebel guns on the hills to their front, Meade prepared to move his line of battle forward.

Preceded by a strong skirmish line which drove the Confederate outposts before them, the long line of Federal soldiers advanced across the open ground toward the woods to their front. Not a shot was fired from the silent woods until the main line was within 800 yards of the waiting Confederate gunners. Colonel Walker gave the signal to fire, and the fourteen guns on Prospect Hill opened up on the advancing Federals. The impact staggered Meade's line which, after slowing its advance, began to waver and then finally came to a complete halt. The fifteen-gun grand battery under Pelham crossed its fire with Walker's guns, increasing the effectiveness of the bombardment.[14] Meade withdrew his men a short distance to the same crest of ground behind which Gibbon's men were sheltered. The Federal artillerists opened fire on the Confederate batteries with a furious counter-bombardment. Every gun which could be brought to bear pounded Prospect Hill and Pelham's position. The enemy battery which was emplaced in advance of the railroad was also battered by Gibbon's divisional batteries. The Federal troops, although sheltered from this artillery fire from the front, were vulnerable to the cross fire coming into their ranks from the advanced Rebel batteries on the left and right.

The punishing blows of the Federal artillery finally silenced the Rebel guns after an exchange lasting over thirty minutes, ending finally about 12 noon.[15] The batteries on Prospect Hill suffered such heavy casualties among the battery teams that the Rebel gunners called their position Dead Horse Hill.

The coolness of the Union artillerymen under the heavy Rebel fire is demonstrated by an incident involving Captain James A. Hall of the Second Maine battery. Captain Hall was sitting quietly on his horse discussing the situation with two of the regimental commanders when a Rebel shell whistled by and crashed into one of Hall's caissons, exploding it. Captain Hall looked annoyed at this interruption and, according to an eyewitness:

> He got down deliberately from his horse, walked over to one of his guns, and sighted it; raised his hand, and an iron missile sped for the mark; a crash and a roar, and in the midst of the Rebel battery there was a sudden upheaval of bursting shells, wheels, splinters, and human flesh. The captain returned to his horse, mounted, and went on with the interrupted talk.[16]

During the height of this second artillery action, General Franklin ordered the First Division of the Third Army Corps to cross the river and support the advance of General Meade. This order was received at 11:30 a.m., and the movement of the division began at once. As these troops arrived on the field, Meade was making the final adjustments in his line before resuming the attack. Brigadier General David B. Birney moved his First Division into the field just to the rear of

Meade's troops, forming each brigade in three lines, the Second Brigade on the right, the Third on the left. The First Brigade was temporarily detained, but when it arrived it was placed in support behind the other two brigades.[17]

Now that Reynolds was sure that Meade's part of the line could be filled in case the attack should fail, he ordered the general advance to begin at 1 p.m. Every battery on the Federal line opened up to cover the movement of the infantry. The Rebel guns concentrated their return fire on the infantry lines, blasting great gaps in them as the Federals advanced across open fields in front of the railroad track. During the initial phase of the assault, the cross fire between the batteries on Prospect Hill and the cavalry guns on the left flank was especially destructive. The Union line was staggered; but this time, after a slight pause, it drove into the heart of the Confederate position. The First Brigade reached the edge of the boggy woods and pushed into the shelter of the trees. Continuing straight ahead, this brigade plunged through the gap left between Archer's and Lane's Brigades. The Third Brigade advanced a little beyond the railroad track before being stopped by gunfire from Archer's and Brockenbrough's men who were still unshaken in their shallow trenches. This fire caused the right regiments of the brigade to sideslip to the right into the woods and placed them on the flank of Archer's troops who were impeding the advance of the rest of the Third Brigade. The Rebel front-line commanders began to call for support from the second line of reserves as they saw the Yankees disappearing into the woods.

Before these calls could be answered, the storm had broken on the reserve brigades of A. P. Hill. Meade's spearhead got clear of the spur of woods at the railroad track and, with only skirmishers in front of it, pushed on toward the crest of the hill. The first organized opposition to appear was Brigadier General Maxcy Gregg's Brigade of South Carolinians. His troops were lying on the ground trying to protect themselves from the Union artillery shells which were crashing through the trees into their position. Their arms were stacked as if they believed the enemy was far away. As soon as the first wave of Meade's men saw the unsuspecting Rebels, they sent a volley into their ranks and then with a cheer rushed forward to break through them. The Rebels gave way for only a short distance before turning and making a stand. The advance of the Federals, however, had already carried a little beyond the military road to the crest of the high ground which they had been ordered to seize.

Meanwhile, back on the Confederate front line, a vicious fight raged on the open flanks of both Archer's and Lane's brigades as the flank regiments of the First Brigade peeled off and swung in behind the Confederate front line. Initially, a large number of prisoners were taken from the flank regiments of Archer's Brigade. However, both Confederate commanders quickly adjusted their formation so that the exposed flank was protected, while they continued to maintain their lines against the attack from the front. Confederate reserves finally arrived on the scene in time to turn the tide of battle against the Federals. Thus, despite the fact that Meade's Second Brigade quickly caught up with the stalled advance of the First Brigade, the Union soldiers were unable to make any further headway against the heavy masses of General Early's troops which were streaming down from the rear to stop the Federal breakthrough. A stubborn fight ensued on the side of the hill, while Meade's outnumbered men attempted to hold the ground they had taken until supporting units could come to their assistance.[18]

Almost thirty minutes after Meade had begun his assault, General Gibbon received the signal to seize the woods directly in his path and support Meade's further advance. Gibbon's Second Brigade was launched toward the Rebel line and was met by a withering fire of artillery and musketry which stopped its advance short of the railroad track. The Third Brigade was rushed to reinforce the halted Second Brigade but, after reaching the latter's position, it was also forced to stop. The tremendous fire which cut these brigades to pieces convinced Gibbon that the only way to carry the Confederate line was with the bayonet, so he ordered his last brigade to make this attempt.

Colonel Adrian R. Root's First Brigade advanced at 1:45 p.m. through the broken remnants of the rest of the division.[19] When Root arrived at the point of farthest advance, he found only the Twelfth Massachusetts still contending with the entrenched Rebels. By this time Root's Brigade was suffering as heavy losses as previous units of Gibbon's divison, and his attack threatened to bog down at almost the same spot as the others. But quickly sizing up the situation, Colonel Root and his staff officers got the brigade to continue forward with the bayonet, joined by the Twelfth Massachusetts and small groups from the shattered regiments which had already fallen to the rear. As his troops caught sight of the Rebels in their works, they broke into a run, crossed the railroad track, and swept into Lane's position. Just as Root's Brigade bore down on the Rebel trenches, the regiments opposing him ran out of ammunition and were unable to stop his charge. The Federals pushed through the position and a short distance beyond into the edge of the woods before being forced to a halt by the Confederate reserves coming to Lane's support. Root reported his success to General Gibbon and was ordered to continue the advance. He was promised that support would arrive soon.

The situation rapidly became serious for the men who had made this small penetration in Lane's line, because the Rebels now pushed troops past both of their flanks in an effort to surround them. General Nelson Taylor, who had taken over the brigade command with the wounding of General Gibbon, ordered Root to withdraw when the safety of the brigade required such a move. The threat to his flanks was the final blow to any hope Root may have had of maintaining his position until support arrived. Reluctantly he ordered his men to withdraw to the Old Richmond Road. During this disengagement, his troops suffered heavy losses from the Confederate batteries and infantry fire. The only gain Gibbon's men had to show for their gallant assault was a group of 200 Rebel prisoners taken during the initial minutes of the attack when they had overrun the Thirty-third North Carolina Regiment.[20]

While Gibbon's men were being forced out of the Rebel position, the same fate was befalling Meade's outnumbered regiments. The men fought hand-to-hand along portions of the penetration, hoping to hold long enough for support to arrive, but the superior numbers of Confederates surrounding them on three sides made this impossible. Meade, seeing that unless support was quickly provided his men would be forced to relinquish the gains they had made, sent urgent requests to Birney and Gibbon for help. Gibbon's division launched its abortive attack into the woods on the right of Meade's penetration, although the latter's men were already beginning to withdraw when Root's Brigade overran the Thirty-third North Carolina. This diversion, however, materially aided in the disengagement of Meade's troops. General Birney, after a slight delay, was able to send part of his Second Brigade to assist Meade in the withdrawal, but these men became mixed up with the troops already in the pocket and were of little practical assistance. It was 2:15 p.m. when General Hardie, watching the action from Franklin's Headquarters, saw the first groups of Meade's men come streaming out of the Confederate position. The troops moved at a walk but in no semblance of order. An attempt was made to rally the regiments at the railroad track in order to hold at least part of the gains made in the attack, but this effort proved fruitless. Two of the brigade commanders were out of action, and the units were so disorganized by the wooded terrain over which they had charged that it was impossible to re-form the men for a stand.[21]

The Confederates, having restored the integrity of the main line, pushed on to clear the railroad track of the Federals. Two of the brigades from Ewell's Division impetuously charged into the mass of Meade's disorganized men who broke at the shock and fled to the rear. The Rebels followed the retreating Yankees almost to the Old Richmond Road before the Union batteries and infantry reserves put a stop to their rash pursuit. Every battery on the line concentrated its fire on this small group of Confederates, causing severe losses. When Birney's unshaken brigades poured disciplined volleys into them at close range, the gray-clad troops withdrew to the safety of their own lines.[22] This brief counterattack caused great anxiety on the Federal side because, at the moment it was launched, the hole in the line created by the repulse of both Meade and Gibbon had not been adequately covered by reserve units.

Shortly after General Birney had placed his division in a reserve position prior to the attack, he received permission to retire behind the roadway in order to shelter his men from the artillery fire descending on the open plain forward of the Old Richmond Road. This movement had not yet been completed when Meade made his call for assistance. Part of Brigadier General J. H. Hobart Ward's brigade was sent to assist in the withdrawal, and at the same time two regiments were shifted to the right to support Gibbon's divisional batteries which were now unprotected. The advance of Gibbon's three brigades left that part of the line completely devoid of troops. As the retreating men from Meade's Division passed Birney's position, an attempt was made to rally them on the front line; but the beaten regiments sullenly continued to the rear where they were reorganized by their own officers. The Rebel counterattack was beaten off by Birney who had deployed his three brigades in line to cover the front originally protected by Meade. Gibbon's men, upon their withdrawal, re-formed their shattered ranks just to the rear of the Old Richmond Road where they awaited relief by the Second Division of the Third Corps, ordered across the river to their support a little after 2 p.m. This division moved into position next to Birney's Division, re-establishing the integrity of the defensive line of the Left Grand Division. The front line was moved forward of the Old Richmond Road about halfway to the railroad track and protected by a strong line of skirmishers.[23]

General Smith's Sixth Corps was, to all practical purposes, not utilized during the entire day. The skirmish line was heavily engaged as well as the divisional batteries, but no movements of the divisions were made. A steady cannonade on Smith's troops continued most of afternoon, causing some loss in his exposed ranks; but except for this artillery fire, his men were not participants in the fight. General Bayard and his brigade of cavalry were stationed on the river bank in reserve and were not called on during the afternoon of the heaviest fighting. While he was waiting for orders near Franklin's headquarters, Bayard himself was killed by a long range shot from a Whitworth gun emplaced far on the Union left flank across the Massaponax River.

On the left, Doubleday continued to protect that exposed flank of the army against the repeated threats of Stuart's dismounted cavalry. His skirmish line was driven in several times by determined charges of Rebel sharpshooters but was always re-established by the outpost reserve. Doubleday's batteries were in action against Prospect Hill as well as against Pelham's battery in the plain by the Massaponax River. Captain DeRussey's batteries on the north bank of the river, being in position to enfilade Confederate troops operating against Doubleday's flank, helped to slow up Rebel activities on this front. Enemy batteries and groups of cavalry were dispersed during the day by DeRussey's accurate, long-range fire.[24]

Shortly after 2:30 p.m., when Meade's troops began to stream out of the woods in retreat, General Franklin received an order from Burnside to make a general attack with his whole force. The aide who delivered the message described it in the following words: "Tell General Franklin, with my compliments, that I wish him to make a vigorous attack with his whole force; our right is hard pressed."[25] This order was sent because of the disaster overtaking the assault of Sumner's Grand Division against Marye's Heights back of the city. Burnside hoped to draw off some of the pressure against Sumner by renewing the attack on Franklin's front.

General Franklin did not order this general assault and informed Burnside that he could not comply with his request.[26] At the time the order was received, Reynolds' Corps was either used up or already engaged with the enemy. Smith's Corps, although not seriously engaged at that moment, was in line and, if withdrawn to make an assault, would have uncovered the bridges which were the only means of withdrawal across the river in case of retreat. The two divisions of the Third Corps which had crossed the river to Franklin's support were in line replacing the battered divisions of Meade and Gibbon.

Some hope was expressed that, if Meade's troops could be reorganized in time, a new assault might be made before darkness set in; but this did not prove feasible. Meade's division had already suffered almost 1,800 casualties, amounting to as high as forty per cent of the combat strength of some of the regiments. The morale of the men was still good, but such high casualties had reduced their combat effectiveness to the point that a further assault would have had little chance of success. The heavy pressure exerted by the Confederates along the entire line of skirmishers seemed to indicate that some offensive action by Jackson could be expected. Under these circumstances, Franklin did not feel justified in ordering a general advance of his grand division.[27] He was happy to hold part of what he had gained in advance of the Old Richmond Road while he reorganized the remnants of Meade's and Gibbon's divisions. The afternoon wore on while this reorganization was being accomplished and, by the time the troops were ready for any further offensive efforts, it was too late in the day to launch an attack.

At 3 p.m. Franklin assumed control of Brigadier General William W. Burns's Division of the Ninth Corps which was in position along Deep Run, connecting the flanks of the Right and Left Grand Divisions. This division was placed near the center of the line in order to facilitate its employment by Franklin if the need arose. Fearing for the safety of his three pontoon bridges, in case Smith's lines should give way, Franklin moved Burns across Deep Run and deployed him in front of the vital spans. These troops remained in this position the remainder of the day, securing the line of retreat of the entire Left Grand Division. Later in the afternoon, General Newton's Division of the Sixth Corps, which had been kept in reserve, was shifted to the left to take up a supporting position to the rear of Birney's troops. Newton remained at this point in the line until nightfall brought an end to further military activity on the part of the Confederates.[28]

General "Stonewall" Jackson, having repulsed the two major Federal assaults, determined to launch a counterblow while his enemy was still disorganized. However, the shifting of divisions in the Federal lines led Jackson to think that a new attack was brewing and he waited to receive it. Finally, realizing that Franklin was not going to renew his assault, Jackson issued orders to begin a general counterattack.

Jackson was aware that the superior Federal artillery would wreak havoc in his assaulting columns if allowed to fire unopposed. Therefore, he ordered some of his batteries to precede the infantry line and silence the Federal cannon. This order was late in reaching all the units involved. In fact, many of the front line brigades were mixed up and had not yet re-grouped after the repulse of Meade's men. After a considerable delay, a rather halting movement began along part of the line. A few Rebel guns were rolled clear of the woods into the open ground, only to be met by a storm of fire from the watchful Yankee gunners. This reception convinced Jackson that only disaster could result from pressing the assault and he reluctantly cancelled the attack order. Since most of the infantry were still concealed by the woods when the recall was sounded, the Union commanders were not aware that a Confederate assault had been repulsed almost before it got underway.[29]

On General Stuart's front the order for a general attack was eagerly received and transmitted to the dismounted Confederate troopers. Stuart was to begin his advance upon a signal from the main position. But, as night was beginning to fall, it was difficult to determine whether or not the signal had been given. Finally, as darkness deepened, Stuart, believing that he must have missed the signal, ordered his line forward. His guns were rolled to the front and began a rapid fire on Doubleday's main line. His aggressive troopers moved forward rapidly, with the accompanying batteries frequently changing position to close the range. The Federal line did not give an inch; and, as the Rebels closed the distance, the return fire became hotter and more accurate. Stuart's position was growing desperate when a courier arrived with Jackson's order of recall. Turning about and withdrawing as fast as they had advanced, the cavalrymen returned to their line of departure, covered by the cloak of night.[30] This brought to a close the only Confederate attempt to make a general counterattack in that sector.

With the coming of darkness, the guns on both sides of the line lapsed into silence, broken now and then by a flare-up of firing at one point or another as the gunners fired at the flash of their opponents' weapons. On the skirmish line, a steady rattle of musketry continued for some time after the artillery ceased firing, since both armies, in fear of a night attack, maintained strong picket lines in close proximity to each other. The men in the divisions slept on their arms, ready to defend their portion of the line on a moment's notice.

General Franklin at his headquarters received the reports of the condition of each of his commands and prepared to inform General Burnside of the results of his reconnaissance-in-force.[31] Reynolds' Corps, which contained two of the assault divisions, had suffered a total of over 3,300 casualties during its unsuccessful bid to seize Prospect Hill. Birney's Division of the supporting Third Corps had lost almost a thousand more in extracting Meade from his penetration of the Rebel line. These casualty lists grimly testified that the fighting edge of two of Franklin's best divisions had been lost and would impair their offensive use the next day.[32] Although Meade and his regimental commanders vehemently contended that they could have held their gains if only support had arrived in time, Franklin realized by the aggressive Confederate counterattack which followed that the Rebel position had not been badly shaken. The Union troops had fought well and deserved better success. Some of the regiments had lost over half their strength in the space of less than an hour without breaking. Even when finally forced to retreat, they had left at a walk, not at a run.

Franklin told his subordinates to hold their men in position and await further orders. The medical officers and the ambulance teams brought the wounded lying within the friendly picket line back to the divisional hospitals for treatment. Hundreds of the less fortunate casualties were forced to spend the whole night between the edgy picket lines and do without medical aid.[33]

With the fighting of the day ended, the men of Franklin's Left Grand Division, exhausted though they were, had to carry out the army routine of re-supply and evacuation.

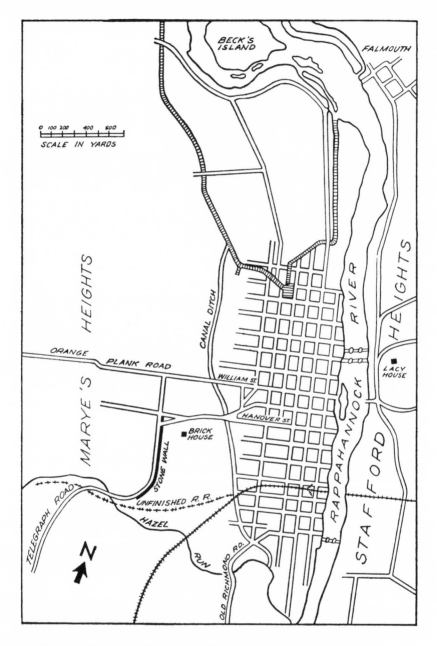

MAP 7 — Fredericksburg and Vicinity
Based on Plate XXXII, No. 5, *Atlas to Accompany the Official Records.*

CHAPTER IX

SUMNER AND THE STONE WALL

Fredericksburg presented a dismal appearance on the morning of December 13. Only a few hardy civilians remained, and most of the buildings in the city were deserted. The effects of the bombardment on the eleventh had left the normally tidy city a shambles. Most of the structures were still standing, but the streets were cluttered with bricks and tile from the roofs, as well as all kinds of abandoned furniture and spoil left by the looting soldiery. Most of the flammable material from the houses had been removed for camp fires.[1] The streets were packed with the soldiers of General Sumner's Right Grand Division. Artillery batteries were parked wherever space permitted, and there was a constant parade of staff officers and couriers going back and forth. At the bridgeheads, members of the provost guard refused passage to any without passes, and looters were separated from their booty before being returned under guard to their regiments. Soon large stacks of property were collected at the head of each bridge waiting for the owners to claim them.[2] A thick fog still blanketed the city when General Burnside's attack order was delivered to General Sumner at his Lacy House headquarters.

While the Federal soldiers in Fredericksburg cooked their breakfast and their officers studied the attack order, the Confederates on the hills back of the city made final adjustments in their lines. This portion of the front was held by Lieutenant General James Longstreet and his Second Army Corps. Longstreet's line ran from Taylor's Hill in the north to Deep Run in the south, where his flank connected with Jackson's Corps. The five divisions of the Second Corps were deployed with Anderson's Division occupying the high ground from Taylor's Hill along the ridge to the Plank Road; McLaws' Division from the Plank Road south across Hazel Run to Howison Hill; Pickett's and Hood's Divisions dividing the defense of the Lansdown Valley, with Hood tying in to Jackson's flank at Deep Run. Ransom's Division was placed in reserve on Marye's Heights.

The front-line Confederate brigades went into position along the lower slopes of the ridgeline, taking cover behind hastily erected field

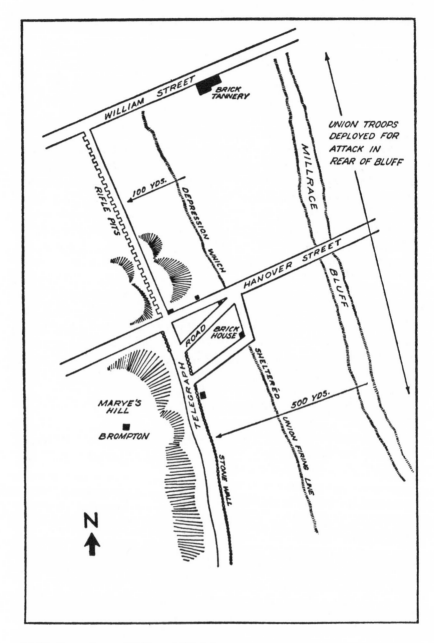

MAP 8 — Stone Wall and Vicinity
Based on map of Fredericksburg, *The National Atlas,* p. 374.

works. Some trenches and gun pits were dug, and natural obstacles such as stone fences were incorporated in the line. But here, as on Jackson's front, the strength of the position lay in the clear fields of fire and the concealment of the woods on the ridge. Topographically, the most vulnerable portion of the line was the southern end of Marye's Heights. This portion of the ridge consisted of Marye Hill, on which stood the beautiful home, "Brompton," and Willis Hill, which ended abruptly at Hazel Run. This portion of the ridgeline was only 600 yards from the edge of the city, providing a partially covered approach for assaulting columns. The ridge to the south, starting with Lee's Hill, was farther back from the river, so that Marye and Willis Hills jutted out from the main Confederate line, forming a salient toward the enemy.

Superficially, this made it appear easy to reach by a determined effort. However, on close inspection, the position was abnormally strong.[3] The Rebels placed batteries of artillery at intervals along the ridge to bear on the town and the plain in front of the high ground. At Stansbury and Cemetery Hills north of the salient, batteries were located so that they could fire almost directly into the flank of units moving from the town to Marye Hill. On the right, a similiar situation existed. The batteries on Lee's and Howison Hills, as well as two large Parrotts, were emplaced to sweep the ground in front of the salient. On the brow of the salient itself, a nine-gun battery of the Washington Artillery under Colonel J. B. Walton was in position to fire point-blank into any forces moving to the assault.[4]

In addition to the heavy concentration of artillery both on the flanks and the face of the salient, there was one other feature which made this position exceptionally formidable. Telegraph Road ran along the base of both Marye and Willis Hills, turning at the end of Willis Hill and running along the Hazel Run Valley a short distance before curving southwest again to follow a route behind the main ridgeline. This road had been cut from the edge of the ridgeline and the roadbed was below the level of the surrounding plain. On both sides of the roadway, stone retaining walls had been built, thus affording potential defenders a prepared intrenchment. The ground sloped gently away from the stone wall toward the city. There was one small depression in this slope about 100 yards from the Rebel line. Another more severe fold in the ground occurred just west of the millrace and bisected the open plain to the rear of the city about 300 yards from the edge of the buildings. The nearest stone wall was built in such a way that only the top portion of it showed above the surface of the slope so that, when the first assaults were made, the Federals did not suspect the existence of the position nor appreciate its strength.[5]

Brigadier General Thomas R. R. Cobb's Brigade was positioned in this sunken road to protect the battery of Colonel Walton on the plateau above. Originally, the Confederates intended to hold this position only as a picket line, but after closer examination they decided to incorporate it into the main defenses. The stone wall which began opposite the end of Willis Hill ended at Hanover Street, and from that point a rifle trench was dug to cover the front between Hanover Street and the Plank Road farther to the left. A small cluster of houses, the most conspicous of which was a two-story brick house, stood about 100 yards in front of the stone wall at the juncture of Hanover Street and Telegraph Road.[6]

When fully manned, this part of the line, with its made-to-order stone walls, was obviously one of the strongest points in the Confederate defense. Officers and men alike expressed confidence in the position. During an inspection trip to this line, General Longstreet asked the reserve artillery commander, Colonel E. P. Alexander, if more artillery ought not to be emplaced. The colonel replied, "General, we cover that ground now so well that we will comb it as with a fine-tooth comb. A chicken could not live on that field when we open on it."[7] Longstreet, who was at his best when fighting a tactically defensive battle, hoped the Yankees would not disappoint him by attacking only the sector under the care of "Stonewall" Jackson.

General Sumner, after receiving Burnside's attack order, notified Major General Darius N. Couch to begin the attack with his Second Corps. The point of attack was the major deciding factor in choosing this corps, since Couch's divisions were directly opposite the objective of the Right Grand Division. Couch was instructed to make his attack with one division, supported by at least one other, in a push for the heights up the Plank and Telegraph Roads. The tactical plan was to cover the forward movement with a cloud of skirmishers to drive in the enemy pickets and follow this movement by the mass of the attacking division, so that the retiring pickets and the assault elements would arrive at the enemy position at the same time. If this could be accomplished, the Federals would be on top of the defenses before any effective fire could be brought to bear against them. Although this method of assault was theoretically excellent, it was most difficult to execute.

Since General French's Third Division was in position nearest the outskirts of the city, he was given the order to prepare his men for the assault. He received this order at 8:30 a.m. and immediately began his preparations. From houses at the edge of the city, there was a clear view of the open plain, and through prior observation French was familiar with the major terrain obstacles in his path. The first problem was to get across the millrace ditch which traversed the plain about 150 yards beyond the outskirts of the town.[8] A regiment had gone the previous day to the mill and had raised the gates in an attempt to lower the water level in the spillway.[9] This proved partially successful, but the ditch remained unfordable along most of its course. The ditch itself was fifteen feet across and five to six feet deep. Bridges were available at each of the street crossings, but these would canalize the movement of the assault columns, making them particularly vulnerable at these points. On the enemy side of the ditch, however, a sharp rise protected the troops during deployment into their attack formations. Beyond the rise, other obstacles stood in the way of the assault formations. Near the junction of Hanover Street and Telegraph Road, the cluster of houses located just short of the first line of Rebel trenches and a series of high board fences crisscrossing the open plain would break up the integrity of the brigade battle lines as they moved to the attack.

The attack formation was prescribed by General Sumner as a column of brigades formed at 200-yard intervals. This formation consisted of each brigade in a long line two ranks deep, moving one behind the other at a specified distance.[10] Such an arrangement was designed to maintain the momentum of the forward movement in an assault. If the leading brigade was stopped by the fire of the defenders, the next brigade in the column could sweep through the stalled unit and carry forward into the enemy position. The chief disadvantage of this method lay in the disorganization of the succeeding waves as they passed to the front.

All necessary arrangements for the assault were completed by General French shortly before 11 a.m., and he reported to headquarters that his division was prepared to move forward. General Couch also notified General Sumner that his corps was ready whenever the commander should give the word. The heavy fog had lifted an hour earlier, and the combatants could now see each other clearly, but only scattered firing indicated the location of the picket line, the main forces remaining passive for the time being.

General Burnside was anxiously waiting for some word of Franklin's bid to seize the south end of the heights and get behind the right flank of the Confederate position. He had received reports of the beginning of Meade's movement downriver; but, except for the muted sound of sporadic gunfire on his left, he received no information concerning the progress of the attack.[11] At 10:30 a.m., becoming impatient at the delay, he sent an aide to Franklin to determine his exact situation, particularly which units were engaged.[12] Before this officer could return with the information, Burnside made an unfortunate decision. As he indicated in his report, "Feeling the importance of haste, I now directed General Sumner to commence his attack."[13]

By ordering Sumner to make his attempt against Marye's Heights before he learned whether Franklin had been successful on the left, Burnside completely abandoned his battle plan. His original order plainly indicated that Sumner's attack was to be made only after the blow by the Union left had succeeded in shaking the Confederates to the point where a power punch into the strong Marye's Hill position would have a good chance of succeeding. Burnside never explained his change of plan, other than by indicating that Franklin was taking so much time that he feared that daylight would run out before he could launch Sumner's attack. It is probable that this change in plan was really brought on by Burnside's lack of confidence in his own abilities. Aware that his army was in a disadvantageous position, and that his original plan required an initial success if it were to work, the unexplained delay of the first attack until late in the morning may well have made him desperate. The nearness of the enemy position and the confidence he undoubtedly felt in the abilities of the thousands of Union troops massed in Fredericksburg probably tipped the scales in favor of an immediate assault. It was certainly a gamble that might pay off, but the risk was great. If the assault failed, it would certainly be at a high cost in casualties for nothing.

Once Burnside's decision to attack was transmitted to General Sumner, only minutes passed before the troops, already formed, began their rush for the heights. General French's division was the first to move forward.[14] At almost the same instant, General Longstreet turned to his artillery commander and ordered the batteries to open fire on the city streets leading to the Confederate position, thereby creating a diversion in favor of the Confederate right.

The Union and Confederate batteries opened fire almost simultaneously. The Federal guns in position on Stafford Heights pounded the Rebel batteries and troop positions as long as possible, but they had to shift their fire higher up on the slopes when the infantry debouched from the city. The fuses for the Federal shells were so unreliable that many of the batteries were forced to resort to solid shot in order to protect their own infantry from the "soon explosions," as Captain Otto Diedrichs of the First New York Artillery called them.[15] The return fire of the Rebel gunners swept the streets of Fredericksburg with both solid shot and shell, disrupting the movement of the assault columns on the way to the attack. Men in the waiting regiments of Hancock's Division were cut down in the streets by the exploding shells as they hugged the sides of the buildings seeking shelter. The entire city of Fredericksburg was dominated by the Confederate batteries and no place in the city was immune from attack. The presence of Confederate sharpshooters on the picket line just outside the town made it impossible to plant any field batteries on the edge of Fredericksburg until the picket line was driven in.[16]

A strong body of skirmishers under Colonel John S. Mason emerged from the city just as the first of Longstreet's guns opened on the town. The force, 700 strong, left the protection of the buildings via Hanover Street on the right and Prussia Street on the left, crossed the bridges over the millrace, and deployed to the right and left to form the skirmish line. During this movement, the two wings of the skirmish formation were subjected to a severe artillery and small arms fire which caused numerous casualties before the ditch had been crossed. The troops resolutely pushed forward until they occupied the ground on the enemy side of the millrace and could take advantage of the cover provided by the small bluff on the far bank of the ditch. The dash across the open ground had tired the men, and a short halt was ordered while the troops caught their breath.

The Confederate sharpshooters were quickly driven in by this aggressive attack; and, by the time the skirmishers moved into the open again, there were no Rebel soldiers between the advancing line and the main Confederate position. As the Union skirmishers left the shelter of the bluff and moved forward, their ranks were thinned by a concentrated cannon fire from the front and right flank. When the remnants of the force were about 100 yards from the stone wall, a tremendous volley of musketry from behind the wall completely stopped the Federals. The ragged line of sharpshooters threw themselves on the ground, taking advantage of the slight cover afforded by a small rise of ground to their front, and began to return as best they could the fire of the Rebels. Some of Colonel Mason's men on the right took position in the cluster of buildings near the intersection of Hanover Street and Telegraph Road, from which they opened a scattering but accurate fire on the partially exposed gunners of Walton's Washington Artillery on the plateau above the stone wall.[17]

As the skirmish line cleared away the Rebel outposts, the First Brigade of French's Division, under Brigadier General Nathan Kimball, moved onto the plain from the southern end of the city. The regiments moved by the flank past the railroad depot on Prussia Street, across the bridge at the millrace, and then deployed to the right to form a line of battle behind the skirmish line. From the moment Kimball's troops passed the railroad depot, they were under an accurate artillery fire which cut down many of the men before they had even crossed the ditch. A temporary respite was obtained when the bluff on the opposite side of the millrace was reached, under cover of which the brigade line of battle was re-formed. As soon as the regiments were in line, the order to advance was again given, and the Blue line surged forward. The men did not fire a shot as they advanced on the double with fixed bayonets, but bent their heads against the storm of fire raining down on them from the heights. When the remains of Kimball's command were just short of the line of skirmishers, the Confederates behind the stone wall again delivered a withering blast of point-blank rifle fire. The Federal line wavered, then surged up into the gaps of the skirmish line and opened fire on the Rebels, but was unable to move further.

Kimball's line now rested its right at the cluster of houses on Hanover Street; its left, near the unfinished railroad grade which extended from the railroad depot to the southern edge of Willis Hill. The momentum of Kimball's charge had been broken by the muddy ground over which his men had to charge, as well as by the necessity to tear down by brute force several wooden fences which stood in the way of the advance. He had closed to within 100 yards of the stone wall, but his worn troops could get no closer. They hugged the ground along the shallow crest, returned the Confederate fire, and attempted to pick off the gunners of the Rebel batteries. Between Kimball's new line and the city, the route of his attack was marked by dead and wounded, representing almost one-fourth of his command.[18]

Once French's assault began, the various attack waves came quickly, one behind the other.[19] The Third Brigade, commanded by Colonel John W. Andrews, was next. While the Confederate infantry was still volleying into Kimball, the Rebel cannoneers shifted their fire to Andrews' unit as it swarmed out of the city. Following in the footsteps of the First Brigade past the depot and then across the bridge to the shelter of the bluff, the men of the Third pressed forward. Again the advance carried up to, but not beyond, the point reached by Kimball, where the troops once more were stopped by the tremendous firepower generated by the men of Cobb's Brigade behind the stone wall. In addition to these men, the Confederates had moved a new brigade into position on the plateau above the stone wall where they could supplement Cobb's firepower. The men of the Third Brigade in turn opened fire on the enemy entrenchments when they found it impossible to advance into the works themselves.[20] They pushed forward into the firing line and fired at the small targets presented by the Rebels as they bobbed up above the wall long enough to aim and shoot. The Third had hardly got into position before the Second Brigade, under Colonel Oliver H. Palmer, topped the crest of the bluff and came surging in to the attack. Subjected to the same artillery harrassment and the heavy volleys of rifle fire, this brigade suffered the fate of the previous two. Stopped short of their goal, they had no alternative but to try to take by fire what they could not take by assault.

The men of all the regiments which had crossed that fatal field were now so mixed that the three brigade battle lines looked like one very heavy skirmish line.[21] The firing continued unabated and added clouds of smoke to obscure the battlefield. General Couch had taken a position in the tower of the Court House as an observation post. From this vantage point, he could see the entire panorama of the combat at a glance. What he saw in the first few seconds made a deep impression on him; as he perceived the thinned ranks of his Third Division piling up in front of the stone wall, he exclaimed, "Oh great God! see how our men, our poor fellows, are falling!"[22]

French's Division had been stopped with over 1,000 casualties and, with no additional forces to commit, General Couch now sent General Hancock's Division forward to carry the assault into the enemy's works. In order to support Hancock's dash across the plain, two batteries of field artillery were placed in position at the edge of the city to fire on the Confederate guns on the opposite heights. The exposed position of these Federal guns led to high casualty rates among the gun crews with no compensating damage to the enemy. The gallant artillerymen kept to their posts, however, and continued the vain attempt to silence the Rebel guns which were decimating the Union infantry regiments charging across the open ground.[23]

Hancock's Third Brigade, under Colonel Samuel K. Zook, moved forward from the edge of the city at about 12:30 p.m., utilizing three parallel streets, with the left of the brigade passing in front of the railroad depot. The troops were again subjected to accurate cannon fire as they moved through the streets toward the millrace. The regiments that crossed on the bridges above the depot found the planks taken up and were forced to cross on the stringers, which prolonged the ordeal of moving by the flank under a heavy artillery fire. Once on the plain under the cover of the bluff, the brigade line of battle was formed with the right resting on Hanover Street and the left on the unfinished railroad. As soon as this line was formed, the order to attack was given and the men of the Third surged over the crest of the bluff and came into view of the waiting Confederates. The volleys came from behind the stone wall with redoubled fury as fresh regiments were sent to assist Cobb's Brigade. To the advancing Federals, it looked as if the wall were topped by a continuous line of flame which seemed to melt away their ranks, but Zook's regiments would not stop. Upon reaching the farthest point of advance marked by the thick line of Federal soldiers firing from the prone position, Zook's Brigade swept over the reclining troops and pressed on toward the wall. The Confederate fire grew even fiercer, blasting great gaps in the line of battle, and finally brought it to a halt less than twenty-five yards from the wall. When the attack stalled, the troops moved back to the slight crest under which French's men were taking cover and there held their ground, waiting for support. The enemy's fire was returned as long as ammunition remained, then bayonets were fixed, and the men waited for the Rebels to make an attempt to dislodge them. The final surge of Zook's men carried as close to the final objective as any Union attempt that day.[24]

General Lee, from his vantage point south of Marye's Heights, watched the steady and repeated charges of the Federals with a growing uneasiness. Turning to Longstreet, he voiced the fear that the masses of Unionists would break through his line. Longstreet, whose belief in the impregnability of the Marye's Heights position was confirmed by the hundreds of Federal dead and wounded dotting the plain to his front, confidently asserted: "If you put every man now on the other side of Potomac on the field to approach me over the same line, and give me plenty of ammunition, I will kill them all before they reach my line."[25] Despite this confidence, Longstreet ordered Kershaw's Brigade to reinforce the men holding the stone wall, thus placing men four deep behind that position. This massing of defenders resulted in one of the most concentrated and rapid volumes of musketry to be generated by any defense force during the entire war. The Confederate artillery rendered great service during the advance of the attackers, but it was the continuous volley of musketry that finally brought each Union brigade to a complete halt.[26]

As in French's assault, Hancock's brigades succeeded each other in rapid order. Brigadier General Thomas Meagher with his famous Irish Brigade followed Zook. These Irish regiments had to fight without their regimental flags because the old colors had been sent to New York to be exchanged for new flags donated by a group of patriotic Irish citizens. Since the new flags had not yet arrived, General Meagher told his men to place sprigs of green in their caps to remind them of their homeland and the Irish heritage of bravery. Meagher moved his men past the depot and across the millrace under a hail of fire, his regiments impeded in their deployment by the muddy ground. When the Irish Brigade crossed the crest and came into view of the Confederates, it was met by a tremendous shower of musket balls and shell fragments. As the line came nearer to the Confederate position, the Irishmen in the ranks of Cobb's Brigade recognized their fellow countrymen; but though it was a distasteful task, they cut down Meagher's boys with as deadly an aim as they had used to repulse the preceding brigades. The Irish Brigade reached the same point as its predecessors and, like them, was stopped short of the stone wall. The men took what cover was available, in line with the brick house, and began firing to the front.

While portions of Meagher's regiments stayed on the front line until the end of the day, remnants of the brigade withdrew in small groups to the safety of the town. The Irish Brigade was not alone in this partial withdrawal, since fugitives from all the attacking units streamed to the rear following the arrival of each new brigade on the field. The mixing of units, as well as the heavy casualties among the officer personnel, led to a disintegration of discipline and organization. As new units advanced to the attack, many of those already on the firing line assumed they were being relieved; when the assaulting troops passed to the front, these men retired to re-group in Fredericksburg. Twenty-four hours after the combat of December 13, the Irish Brigade was able to muster only 280 men out of the 1,200 sent into battle. The final losses tabulated for this unit, however, were only 545, which indicates that for every casualty there was one man still missing from the brigade the next day.[27]

Into this confused situation, the last brigade of Hancock's Division, under Brigadier General John C. Caldwell, plunged with determination. The appearance of this new brigade brought a redoubled fire from the Rebel batteries on the hills behind Fredericksburg. The Confederate gunners already having determined the accurate range from their positions to the exits from the town, greeted the fresh regiments with a telling fire of solid shot and shell. Caldwell's men suffered like the preceding troops, but they bravely formed their line of battle and moved forward toward the enemy's defenses. When his forces approached the line of survivors still doggedly holding their ground in front of the stone wall, some of his men took what cover was available and, following the example of the troops already there, began to fire. Caldwell could see that if his men stopped where they were, nothing would be accomplished and he rode down his line urging the men onward. By constant exhortation and example, the brigade inched forward a few yards through the mass of men sheltered behind the small crest, but they were finally stopped well short of their goal. On the right Caldwell's men had moved north of Hanover Street in an attempt to flank the stone wall, but the terrific fire of the defenders kept them at a distance.[28] Although the troops could not reach the stone wall, they maintained their line of battle until it was literally carried away by the storm of fire concentrated on it by all the Confederate weapons that could be brought to bear.

Caldwell's First Brigade lost 952 men, with most of the casualties being suffered in the few short minutes it took to cross the open field. In some of the regiments, losses were especially severe. The Fifth New Hampshire went into action with 266 officers and men, but after the fight it could muster only sixty-three men and three officers.[29] Some idea of the tremendous volume of fire which was concentrated to cover the approaches to the stone wall can be gained from the report of the commanding officer of the 145th Pennsylvania Infantry regiment: "Our State flag was pierced with eighteen bullets; our regimental flag with thirteen bullets and one piece of railroad iron, whilst the flagstaff was shattered to pieces with a piece of shell."[30]

The Federals had now completed what was, in effect, six separate assaults on the stone wall position, all of which were brought to a halt by the continuous volleys of musketry from the relative safety of that bastion. The divisions of French and Hancock, or rather what was left of these divisions, were intermixed on a line running from a point just to the right of Hanover Street, parallel to the Confederate line at a distance of about 100 yards, to a point about 150 yards to the left of the railroad embankment leading past Willis Hill.[31] The men sought the slight protection of the small rise in the ground and kept up a desultory fire on the Rebels until all their ammunition had been expended, including the ammunition of the dead and wounded lying within reach.

It had taken just one hour for the first two divisions of the Second Corps to deploy, attack, and recoil from the stone wall. At 1 p.m. General Couch ordered French and Hancock to carry the enemy's works by storm. But, seeing almost at once that this order could not be carried out, he decided to commit his last division. The Second Division, commanded by Brigadier General Oliver O. Howard, was in position along the northern half of Fredericksburg. His mission was to hold the right half of the city and by so doing protect the flank of the corps assault. Couch first ordered Howard to move his division to the right of Hanover Street in order to assist the advance of the stalled units of French and Hancock by flanking part of the stone wall position. The terrain to the right of Hanover Street permitted such a movement. However, before the new troops could begin this maneuver, the orders were cancelled.

While Howard began his deployment to the right of the path followed by French and Hancock, those officers sent urgent appeals to General Couch for support. Their commands were melting away under the heavy fire poured on them from the Confederate defenses. Couch then issued new instructions to Howard to send his division to the support of the stalled units via the same route that they had followed in their assault.[32] This order required a further shift of the attacking elements to the left so that the leading brigade could advance toward the heights on Hanover Street. This unit, under the command of Colonel Joshua T. Owen, was met by a fierce artillery fire as it crossed the millrace. Disregarding the losses caused by the artillery, the brigade pushed on down Hanover Street until it was within 400 yards of the Rebel line. At this point the troops deployed into line of battle to the left of Hanover Street. With the deployment complete, Colonel Owen, now on foot since his horse had been shot from under him, ordered his men forward. The brigade line advanced steadily toward the stone wall, only to find when they had arrived at the small cluster of buildings at the fork of Hanover Street that the units they were ordered to support had virtually ceased to exist. Perceiving that under the circumstances little was to be gained by the slaughter of his men,

Owen ordered the troops to lie down and to return the fire of the Rebels only when they could see a target at which to fire. Colonel Owen reported to General Howard that unless more infantry and artillery were sent, the assault would fail.[33]

Colonel Norman J. Hall was following with his Third Brigade and had halted briefly at the edge of the city so that Owen's Brigade could deploy and take up the proper distance between the attacking waves. Generals Couch and Hancock met Hall at this point and ordered him to charge up Hanover Street in column in an effort to carry the position by sheer mass. Hall deployed his column in the roadway with a front as wide as the road would accommodate. As soon as this dense column of attack appeared on the edge of the city, it became the target of all the Confederate guns that could be brought to bear. The first shells had hardly burst over the heads of the hurrying troops when General Couch, sensing the slaughter which would result if the formation were maintained, directed Hall to deploy to the right of Hanover Street in a regular brigade line of battle and press the attack in this manner. The deployment was completed under a hail of fire, not without some confusion resulting from the change in orders, but finally the line was formed, and moved toward the enemy rifle pits that extended the stone wall defense. The brigade advanced over the bluff at the millrace and moved about halfway to the enemy line, when two of the regiments broke under the severe flanking fire delivered by Confederate batteries on the right. The officers, after some delay, were able to re-establish the line for a second try, during which Hall's men came up on line with Owen's Brigade on the left of the road. Some of the men took position in some houses a few yards from the rifle pits and from this cover sniped at the Rebel trenches. Hall sent word that he could hold his position but could not advance. He was ordered to hold what he had gained.[34]

The severity of the fire directed at Hall's Brigade is shown by the fact that of the 800 men taken into the assault by this unit, more than 500 were lost as casualties. The brigade remained in this forward position during the remainder of the day, exposed to constant fire. Not only did Hall's troops suffer from the projectiles of the enemy but also from the short rounds of their own batteries on Stafford Heights.[35]

The remaining brigade of Howard's Division was held on the edge of the city ready on order to support either of the engaged units. Soon Hall called for reinforcements since his ammunition was getting low. Whereupon Brigadier General Alfred Sully sent two regiments to Hall's support and later sent an additional regiment to back up Owen's line. The remainder of Sully's Brigade was kept under cover near the edge of the city, ready for any eventuality.[36]

With the failure of Colonel Hall's charge, the last offensive power of Couch's Second Corps was expended in a vain effort to reach Marye's Heights. The ground in front of the objective was covered with the bodies of over 4,000 members of the corps who had fallen in the unsuccessful advances made by French, Hancock, and Howard. The remainder of the corps, less the few regiments of Sully's Brigade still in support positions, were either doggedly holding their place behind the low crest less than 100 yards from the stone wall or slipping back to the safety of the city. The confusion of units along the firing line, coupled with the successive charges by one brigade after another, led to the withdrawal of many small segments of preceding regiments. Many others helped wounded comrades to the hospitals in the city and then either lost their way or chose to remain in the city rather than take their chances on the naked plain once more. General Couch, from his vantage point in the tower of the Court House, described the eight brigade charges by his Corps in the following words:

> There was no cheering on the part of the men, but a stubborn determination to obey orders and do their duty. I don't think there was much feeling of success. As they charged the artillery fire would break their formation and they would get mixed; then they would close up, go forward, receive the withering infantry fire, and those who were able would run to the houses and fight as best they could; and then the next brigade coming up in succession would do its duty and melt like snow coming down on warm ground.[37]

So far, Longstreet had been justified in the confidence he had expressed to Lee: that as long as his ammunition held out all the Bluecoats on the other side of the Potomac could not breach his position. The repeated assaults of the Federals, however, had begun to take a respectable toll of the defenders. General Cobb fell mortally wounded early in the engagement, and his place was taken by General Kershaw when that officer brought his brigade to reinforce the troops behind the stone wall. Although not seriously concerned for the safety of his position, Longstreet at 2 p.m. shifted two brigades from Pickett's Division to the left. One brigade was placed in reserve back of Marye's Hill, just in case one of the Union attacks effected a lodgement within his lines, and the other was placed in that portion of the front line vacated by Kershaw's brigade when it went to the assistance of Cobb's men. After the first enemy attacks had been bloodily repulsed, the riflemen behind the stone wall were sure that the Union attack would be shifted to another portion of the position; but the Federal brigades stubbornly continued to debouch from the city and advance over the millrace bluff. In view of the slaughter which resulted, Rebel marksmen, while doubting the enemy's wisdom, could not help marveling at his bravery.[38] General Longstreet, in turn, confidently watched the waves of enemy infantry sweep from the town to their destruction, while his own troops, sheltered from return fire by a slight slope, fired on the attacking forces.[39]

While Couch was unsuccessfully trying to push his brigades up the Hanover Street axis toward the stone wall, Brigadier General Orlando B. Willcox, commanding the Ninth Corps, was standing by to assist him on his left. The Ninth Corps was the connecting link between Sumner's and Franklin's Grand Divisions. On the morning of the battle, these troops were deployed between Hazel Run and Deep Run, holding the center of the Federal line. Once the combat had started, however, the two assaults on either end of the Union line acted as magnets pulling the Ninth Corps units from the quiet central front. Burns's Division shifted to the left to protect the bridges which remained under Franklin's control throughout the battle. The remaining two divisions, however, were ordered to the support of Couch's Second Corps. Just before French's Division began its assault, Brigadier General Samuel D. Sturgis moved his division across Hazel Run into the southern edge of the city. The troops were sheltered among the houses, and a position for a battery of horse artillery was selected on a steep bluff to the left of a brick works on the outskirts of the city. This position was also to the left of the railroad depot which most of Couch's brigades passed on their way to deploy on the open plain.[40]

Brigadier General Edward Ferrero with his Second Brigade rested in position near the brick kilns under a sporadic cannonade from the enemy. The loud reports of the solid shot striking the kilns and sending loose brick flying in all directions caused one unnerved private to remark: "Oh dear! they'll kill every one of us: not a d-d one of us will be left to tell the story!"[41] Despite this dire prediction, the brigade was still intact when the repulse of the left of Couch's leading division forced Willcox to order Sturgis to the Second Corps' support. Ferrero moved his troops, except for one regiment protecting the horse battery on the bluff, across the railroad and then onto the plain in front of Marye's Heights. As soon as his brigade was deployed opposite the right center of the stone wall position, he gave the order to advance. At 12:30 p.m., his men swept forward to the assault, having to pass through several board fences on the way. These fences were broken down in places, and the troops pushed through these gaps over the bodies of dead and wounded left from the earlier assaults.[42] Moving under the same heavy fire that the other Union units had experienced, Ferrero's men were finally stopped 200 yards short of the wall, at which point they began to fire volleys of musketry into the Confederate position. The remaining regiment of the brigade was also sent forward after the battery of horse artillery they were supporting was withdrawn because of superior Rebel artillery fire.[43] In an attempt to improve Ferrero's position, General Sturgis committed the First Brigade to take a position to the left of the halted Second Brigade. It was hoped that by angling the new brigade's front, a cross fire could be opened in front of Ferrero's unit, thus assisting his advance.

Brigadier General James Nagle attempted to carry out Sturgis' order, but he found that the rugged terrain along Hazel Run prevented the deployment of his brigade on the left of Ferrero. Communicating this intelligence to Sturgis, his orders were amended, directing him to attack over the same ground the preceding brigade had used in its assault. This order was obeyed amid a heavy enfilading fire from the Rebel batteries on Lee's and Howison Hills. Despite the confusion caused by the loss of many officers and the obstacles which broke the integrity of the formation, Nagle's troops advanced toward the stone wall. Here again valor was repaid in a heavy casualty list. Stopped short of their goal, the troops took what cover they could find and returned the fire of the enemy from a line of battle established in conjunction with Ferrero's Brigade.[44] This line extended opposite the end of Willis Hill, thus placing the entire stone wall position under attack. Sturgis' Division contained only two brigades; therefore, with the commitment of Nagle, the division was entirely engaged. Unable to withdraw without inviting a counterblow, these troops maintained their position until darkness permitted withdrawal into the city. Over 1,000 men fell in the attacks of these two brigades without causing the slightest apparent effect upon the rocklike Confederate defense of Marye's Heights.[45]

With the movement of Burns's Division to the assistance of Franklin and the employment of Sturgis to support Couch's attack, the only unit remaining available to the Ninth Corps commander was the Third

Division under Brigadier General George W. Getty. General Willcox held this division in place near Hazel Run to maintain the center of the Union line and also to protect the southern end of the city.[46]

As the ill-fated divisions of the Right Grand Division advanced into the smoke and thunder in front of the stone wall, room was now created for the forces held in reserve on the opposite bank of the river to cross into the city. At 1:30 p.m., General Burnside ordered General Hooker to move his troops to the support of General Sumner. At this time, Hooker had the three divisions of the Fifth Corps and Brigadier General Amiel W. Whipple's small division of the Third Corps. Whipple's Division was directed to take the place of General Howard's Division which had been protecting the northern half of the city. This portion of the line had been uncovered when Howard had shifted to the left and gone to the assistance of French and Hancock. Whipple placed his First Brigade on the edge of the city to protect the right flank of the army while his Second Brigade was sent to support General Willcox.[47] Whipple's First Brigade, under Brigadier General A. Sanders Piatt, held the right flank for the remainder of the battle. The Second Brigade, under Colonel Samuel S. Carroll, became engaged later in the day under the direction of General Willcox.

The troops of Brigadier General Daniel Butterfield's Fifth Corps were still crossing the river when Hooker was directed to send one division to the support of General Sturgis' hard-pressed brigades. The division crossing the river closest to this part of the line was commanded by Brigadier General Charles Griffin, who moved his men into the southern edge of the city and awaited further orders from the Ninth Corps commander.[48]

General Hooker arrived on the field shortly after 2 p.m. and went to the front to make a personal reconnaissance of the objective his men were to take. A quick look at the wreckage of the ten brigades which had already attempted to pierce the enemy line convinced him that the small force left at his disposal could not accomplish what the entire Second Corps had failed to do. Hooker had been present that very morning while a Confederate prisoner explained to General Burnside and Sumner that the position at the stone wall was impregnable and that the Rebels hoped this point would be attacked. His subsequent visit to the battlefield confirmed the truth of this prisoner's statement, and the testimony of several of Sumner's general officers substantiated Hooker's belief that to continue the assault would be utter folly. The apparent demoralization of the many stragglers milling about in the town led Hooker to fear the results of continued failure. With their backs to the river panic could quickly lead to a catastrophe of major proportions.

Believing that it was his duty to warn his commanding general of the futility of further efforts at this point, he sent an aide to Burnside with a message advising him not to make the attack. The aide quickly returned with a message informing him that the attack must be made. Feeling very strongly on the matter, Hooker rode to his superior's headquarters and attempted to dissuade him from continuing the attack. This trip failed to alter Burnside's resolve, and the order stood.[49] Hooker returned to the field and reluctantly prepared to commit his remaining two divisions.

Burnside's refusal to change his tactical plan intensified the disaster. From the window of his room in the Phillips House, the Union commander could see the waves of his attacking troops make their assault and withdraw in fragments.[50] His balloon observation post, manned by Professor Lowe most of the day, confirmed the futility of the Union attacks. Yet Burnside's only command decision during this phase of the battle was to reaffirm to Hooker the order to continue the assault on the same point.

Time was slipping away. It was after 3 p.m. when Hooker returned to the field from his unsuccessful interview with Burnside. His first move was to employ the Federal artillery more advantageously. During the first attacks a few guns had been placed in position on the edge of the town and had been brought to bear on the Rebel positions with varying degrees of success. But the Union gunners had found it difficult to make an impression on the protected enemy cannon and, conversely, had found themselves peculiarly vulnerable to counter-battery fire. Despite this experience, Generals Hooker and Couch now decided to risk some field guns across the millrace on the top of the bluff behind which the infantry had been deploying. At 3:30 p.m. Captain John G. Hazard's Rhode Island Battery of six 12-pounders thundered across the millrace, wheeled into position within 150 yards of the stone wall, and opened a rapid fire of shell and solid shot on the entrenched Confederates. Hazard was shortly joined by four guns of Captain John D. Frank's New York Battery which took station at Hazard's left rear and added their fire to the barrage.[51] These guns were well within the effective musket range of the defenders and quickly began to suffer from the accurate fire of the Confederate sharpshooters.

While Hazard and his guns attempted to batter a way through the stone wall, Hooker completed the arrangements for his infantry assault. Brigadier General Andrew A. Humphreys was directed to attack with one of his brigades to the right of Hanover Street and the other to the left. Brigadier General George Sykes's Division, consisting entirely of regular troops, was to attack on the right of Humphreys, echeloned to the right rear so that, in case Humphreys' men were repulsed, his division could be shifted to a supporting role. In the smoke and confusion of the combat, Hooker did not know that further to the left, Griffin was also preparing to launch an attack. But by good luck Griffin and Humphreys moved against the enemy line at almost the same moment.[52]

Griffin and his men remained under cover for half an hour after reporting to General Willcox, until he received his orders to engage the enemy. At 3:30 p.m. he was directed to relieve Ferrero's Brigade. Accordingly, he sent his First Brigade to effect the relief, which was accomplished under a heavy fire of cannon and musketry. These troops made no attempt to reach the stone wall; but, of course, the Confederates could not tell the difference between a relief and an attack. Therefore, they greeted these newcomers with the maximum fire-power available. Ferrero pulled his exhausted troops back to the comparative safety of the city, while the fresh troops of Griffin's First Brigade held their place along the slight crest 100 yards short of the Rebel infantry line. An hour passed with only the steady fire of sharpshooters and cannoneers continuing the contest. Finally, as dusk fell, the order to carry the enemy's works was received. Griffin sent Colonel Jacob B. Sweitzer with his Second Brigade forward toward the stone wall. As this unit deployed, Colonel Carroll's Brigade, which had been ordered from Whipple's Division earlier in the afternoon, joined in on the left. The two brigades swept across the open ground under a terrific storm of fire, only to be turned back well short of the stone wall by the galling musketry of the Confederates. The survivors of this charge took cover behind the crest of the rise which the other Union soldiers were using. Like their predecessors, they opened fire at the enemy, now almost completely invisible in the gloom. Griffin's Third Brigade, under the command of Colonel T. B. W. Stockton, was also sent forward over the fireswept ground, only to be forced to halt on a line with the leading brigades of the division. Stockton held his men in position until relieved from the front line after nightfall.[53]

Further to the right, Humphreys' assault got under way at the same time as Griffin's. Colonel Peter H. Allabach had deployed his

Second Brigade to the left of Hanover Street when, at 4:30 p.m., General Humphreys came up to accompany him in his assault. Poor visibility prevented either officer from determining clearly the exact situation into which he was about to lead his raw troops. The men of Humphreys' Division had been in the service only five months, and this was their first attack under fire. As the brigade line advanced to within 300 yards of the stone wall, movement was seen among the Rebel artillery on top of Marye's Hill. A closer look revealed the fact that the Confederate guns were being withdrawn at a gallop. The Federal troops raised a terrific cheer, thinking the crest was to be theirs, and surged forward at a run. But the movement of guns was simply the relief of the Washington Artillery which had exhausted its ammunition and was being replaced by cannon from Colonel E. P. Alexander's reserve artillery battalion. The fresh guns were rushed into the vacated gun positions amid a hail of Federal artillery and rifle shot and opened fire just as the line of Humphreys' infantry was at effective canister range.[54]

Down on the plain, Allabach's men had come up to the rear of the line of troops who were sheltered by the low crest and were firing at the Rebels behind the wall. The green troops followed this example by taking cover themselves and returning the heavy fire received from the defenders. However, the officers of the brigade urged the men forward and, after some effort, were able to get them moving again. This new effort was turned back by the accurate volleys of Kershaw's defense only after the recruits had edged to within fifty yards of the Confederate position.[55]

With the failure of Allabach's assault, Humphreys rode back to join Brigadier General Erastus B. Tyler who was completing the deployment of the First Brigade to the right of Hanover Street. Convinced that only the bayonet could succeed under the circumstances, Humphreys told the men not to fire unless ordered to, and not to stop when they reached the line of prone infantry, but to charge over them and into the enemy's works. With this admonition, he led them forward at the double. As the brigade came up to the Union firing line they were met not only by a withering Confederate fire but also by Union troops who yelled for them to stop and in some cases even used physical force to halt their forward movement. This opposition slowed the attack and, in places, it forced the line of battle into a column, greatly disarranging the attack formation.[56] Continuing the rush, however, Tyler's men pushed to within twenty-five yards of the stone wall, receiving a redoubled fire from the Confederate riflemen which tore great gaps in the line. It was almost completely dark now, and the bright flash of the enemy's muskets poked holes in the night. The troops still on the ground, meanwhile, were returning the Confederate fire with the result that many of Tyler's men were caught in the middle. The flash of muskets both front and rear proved too much for Tyler's new soldiers and their forward movement slowed, then finally stopped altogether.[57] After firing several volleys into the enemy, the whole brigade turned and withdrew to the rear. Humphreys and his officers tried to rally the men on the main firing line; but despite such entreaties, the men continued to retreat until they were under the cover of the bluff at the millrace.[58]

General Humphreys reported his failure to his corps commander and received instructions to withdraw his division from the field. Humphreys was very bitter about the conduct of the men over which his division had been forced to charge and indicated his belief that the attack would have been a success if other troops had not interfered with his men. Others expressed a contrary opinion both as to the actual firing line incident and Humphreys' chance for success. For example, the unit historian of the 106th Pennsylvania of Howard's Division, who was on this part of the line when the attack took place, claimed that not only was there no physical effort made to stop the forward movement, but that instead the troops attempted to force Humphreys' retreating men to stay on the firing line.[59] Regardless of the truth of the matter, it is certain that Humphreys' troops were greatly impeded by the simple physical barrier presented by the mass of soldiers lying directly in their path. It is likely that Humphreys could have reached the stone wall if these troops on the firing line had been withdrawn first. However, the probability of his forcing a significant breach in the Confederate line was slight.

The advance and repulse of Humphreys' Division was so swift that Sykes's Division had not completed its deployment preparatory to joining the assault. Now that darkness had set in, there was no point in sending Sykes into the cauldron. Therefore, his attack was suspended and his men placed on the edge of the city, prepared to block any efforts of the Confederates to launch a counterattack.[60]

On the left of Griffin's point of attack, the last offensive effort of the day began with the movement of General Getty's Division. He received the order to move out at 5 p.m., even though almost complete darkness had settled over the field. Colonel Rush C. Hawkins' First

Brigade led off the attack by moving past the brick kiln and across the railroad track to strike the enemy position at the southern end of Willis Hill. The darkness caused some confusion and loss of alignment during the movement, but it also reduced the effectiveness of the Rebel cannon fire. When the troops arrived within eighty yards of the stone wall, they became visible to the waiting Confederates who poured heavy volleys into them from front and left flank. The dark uniforms of the Federals blending into the darkness had presented difficult targets to the Rebels up to that time; now, however, they were difficult to miss.[61] Hawkins' men pushed almost up to the wall itself, but the fire was too great. In addition, his men began to suffer from the fire of Federal units to their rear. In the panic which ensued, it seemed as if every soldier in the brigade were yelling at the top of his lungs. This fact was noted by the alert Confederates who reported that the last attack was sent reeling back to town actually howling in discomfiture.[62] Hawkins was able to re-form his men along the mill-race, where they awaited further orders.[63]

Colonel Edward Harland came to Hawkins' support but did not go into action. His brigade halted along the railroad embankment and waited for further orders.[64] By now the open plain was so cluttered with broken units and battle debris that it was difficult for a fresh unit to find room to make an uninterrupted assault.

With the repulse of Getty's attack, the Union army suspended its futile, almost suicidal, lunges against the impregnable position on Marye's Heights. The firing continued fitfully for a while, with every discharge of a musket or cannon clearly visible in the now-complete darkness. The day was over, the men had done what they could to achieve victory but had failed. As the last Federal line of battle retreated into the blackness, some of the men could hear a cock crow in triumph from behind the stone wall. Some members of Cobb's Brigade had trained a gamecock to crow on a signal from his owner and, during the conduct of the defense, sent the piercing call of this rooster after each retreating Union brigade. When the last attack was repulsed, it was reported that "the cock, with repeated crows, sounded the victory."[65] For the Federals, there was no victory to celebrate, only individual thankfulness for survival.

Under cover of darkness, the units on the front lines were relieved by Sykes's Division and withdrawn into the city for reorganization.[66] The noise of this movement brought instant fire from the watchful pickets of the enemy, for the Confederates could not be sure but that the Federals might try a night assault to gain their objective. As the various units cleared the field after their relief and a relative quiet settled over the area, men along the front began to hear the disquieting sound of their wounded still lying between the lines, without medical aid. Colonel Joshua L. Chamberlain of the 20th Maine Volunteers described the sound which came to him as he hugged the cold earth during the night of December 13:

> But out of that silence from the battle's crash and roar rose new sounds more appalling still; rose or fell, you knew not which, or whether from the earth or air; a strange ventriloquism, of which you could not locate the source, a smothered moan that seemed to come from distances beyond reach of the natural sense, a wail so far and deep and wide, as if a thousand discords were flowing together into a key-note weird, unearthly, terrible to hear and bear, yet startling with its nearness . . .[67]

Few of these unfortunate men managed to survive until the withdrawal of the contending forces finally permitted help to reach them, two days later.

In the town, an almost indescribable confusion existed. The houses and public buildings were turned into hospitals and filled with the wounded and dying. In the streets, officers attempted to round up the remnants of their commands so they could be re-supplied with ammunition and once more become combat-effective. Few lights were shown because of fear of a Confederate bombardment, which in the city would have inflicted heavy losses on the survivors of the day's assault. Regimental commanders took muster of their troops simply by counting the muskets in the stacks where their men were bivouacking.[68] Now that the excitement of battle was over, some of the commanders began to realize for the first time how heavy their casualties had been. General French, riding through the streets, came across one of his regimental adjutants leaning against a building and exclaimed to him in anguish, "Adjutant, where is my division? Tell me where my men are. My God, I am without a command!"[69]

During the long hours of the night, the units gradually were re-organized and re-supplied, although in some cases the numbers still with the colors were shockingly small. The night was cold and clear and later in the evening the watching Confederates saw strange lights in the sky across the river, which they first assumed to be the reflection of a burning Federal supply dump. As the splendor of the light increased, however, some of the more widely-traveled explained that it was a display of the Aurora Borealis, or Northern Lights, which are seldom seen so far south. The jubilant Rebels professed to see this aerial display in the heavens as a celebration of their victory over the foe.[70]

When the coming of darkness brought an end to the fighting, General Burnside was faced with the indisputable fact that his tactical plan had been a complete and bloody failure. On the left, his attack, though temporarily successful, had in the end been repulsed; on the right, his men had not even set foot within the Confederate position. He crossed the river and visited the troops and commanders on the ground in an effort to determine what steps to take to make up for the failure. After spending most of the night looking over the situation, he returned to his headquarters determined to continue the assault on the stone wall the next morning but with one change in technique: he was going to lead the assaulting column in person.[71]

CHAPTER X

SAVING THE ARMY

General Burnside returned to his headquarters and communicated to Sumner his plan for the renewal of the battle the next morning. He directed Sumner to form the Ninth Corps into a massive column of attack by regiments, to move at daylight, and to attempt by sheer mass to penetrate the stone wall position. Sumner then relayed this order to the officers of the Ninth Corps who were directed to complete the arrangements.[1] Colonel Daniel Leasure, commanding the leading brigade in this attack formation, immediately protested the plan. He pointed out that the loss of life would be very heavy without much chance of success. This protest was seconded by Leasure's division commander and by General Willcox, the Corps commander.[2] The order stood, however, and Burnside indicated to Couch that he was going to lead the charge in person to insure its success.[3] At 4 a.m. Burnside telegraphed to Lincoln the results of Saturday's fighting and concluded with the hope that the crest would be carried the next day.[4] During the few remaining hours of darkness, the Federal army prepared itself for one more try at the Confederate defenses.

The next morning, just before the troops were to move forward, General Sumner approached Burnside and attempted once more to dissuade him. He told him, "General, I hope you will desist from this attack; I do not know of any general officer who approves of it, and I think it will prove disastrous to the army."[5] Such advice from a trusted officer who normally inclined toward offensive operations caused Burnside to postpone the attack while he consulted his other subordinates. All of these officers seconded Sumner's view, including Franklin, who was summoned from his flank of the army for an opinion. The unanimity among his general officers finally persuaded Burnside to rescind his attack order and switch to the defensive temporarily. He indicated that in making this decision he had also been influenced by the words of the President:

Inasmuch as the President of the United States had told me not to be in haste in making this attack; that he would give me all the support that he could, but he did not want the Army of the Potomac destroyed, I felt that I could not take the responsibility of ordering the attack. . . .[6]

When the order was rescinded, the commanders and men designated to make the assault gratefully moved back to their assembly areas, for, although they were ready to obey Burnside's order, they knew it would lead only to more slaughter. Indeed, at that very moment, an even hotter reception was being prepared for them at the stone wall than the one they had gotten the day before. Unknown to the Federals, a courier carrying a copy of the attack order had wandered into the Rebel lines and had been captured. Burnside's order had quickly been placed in Longstreet's hands, and as a result, appropriate preparations were being made for the expected assault.[7] This captured order was, by a strange twist of fate, to aid the Union cause during the remaining two days of the operation by convincing Lee that Burnside had not given up hope of forcing the Confederate position.

Following the cancellation of the attack order, Burnside returned to his headquarters to ponder the possibilities open to his stalled army. Along the battle lines, however, a fitful combat continued. Except directly in front of the stone wall, the two armies were separated by the re-established picket lines along which the usual contention existed.[8]

Late on the preceding evening, General Sykes's Division of regulars had moved to the extreme limits of the advance and had relieved the remnants of Howard's troops, who were still holding tenaciously to the depression just short of the stone wall. Having moved up during the darkness, the men along the front line did not realize their proximity to the enemy until the fog lifted the next morning. The haze suddenly dissipated, and the opposing forces were revealed to each other.[9] The Federals saw the Confederates behind the wall, standing in groups calmly talking or cooking rations, but in an instant the scene changed and not a man could be seen. A volley of shots from the wall convinced the exposed Union regulars that the safest place was flat on the ground. Once there, they were forced by the vigilant Rebel sharpshooters to remain, for any movement was instantly rewarded with an accurately-aimed Minié ball. The shelter of the depression was not more than one foot high in places; therefore, the men were kept in a very cramped position during the remaining daylight hours. The Confederate guns could not depress enough to bear on the advance line, but they could effectively cut off any contact between the advanced regulars and possible help from the rear. Unable to move about, these regulars maintained their position during the long hours of that winter day while the cold muddy ground chilled them to the bone.[10] Ordered not to return the fire of the Confederates, lest a general engagement be precipitated, the long-suffering Federals waited for the setting of the sun to bring an end to their ordeal.

The inactivity was not endured with equal patience by all the exposed troops. Here and there an officer or soldier, goaded to desperation by the experience, would leap to his feet and fire a round at the enemy. More often, he would simply shake his fist at the Rebels and shout his defiance at them before being driven to cover again or riddled with rifle balls. Some of the color bearers made a practice of advancing the colors a few paces and driving them into the ground to show their contempt for the fire of the Confederates.[11] The accurate fire of the concealed marksmen led some of Sykes's men to take possession of a large brick tannery which stood on the right flank of the line next to the Plank Road. The walls facing the enemy position were loopholed, and the Federal sharpshooters were at last able to reply effectively to the Rebel fire. This fire enabled the Federals to suppress much, but not all, of the sniping from behind the stone wall.[12]

In the city, the roundup of stragglers and reorganization of units continued during the day with commanders seeking what shelter was available for the bivouac areas of their units. At noon, the surviving officers of General Meagher's Brigade held a banquet with all the trimmings to celebrate the arrival of the new colors for the Irish Brigade. Amidst the scenes of devastation, these few at least found some distraction from their troubles until a Confederate battery found the range of the hall being used for the occasion. The entrance of several Rebel solid shot into the building dampened the spirits of the celebrants and broke up the party.[13]

Most of the public buildings in the city were not the scene of such happy gatherings. The wounded crowded every corner of the churches and many of the larger homes in Fredericksburg. As soon as immediate surgery was completed, the casualties were carried across to collecting stations on Stafford Heights and from there to the railroad for transportation to the base hospital in Washington.[14] Occasional Confederate cannonading found these hospitals, but this was the result of a few random shots and not a systematic bombardment of the town.

Along General Franklin's lines, the skirmishing was especially bitter during the morning of December 14.[15] The enemy sharpshooters were extremely active and were supported by the fire of numerous batteries whenever any attempt was made by the Union skirmish reserve to push back the outpost line. The firing became so heavy that General Hardie sent several messages to Burnside from Franklin's headquarters indicating that they were awaiting a general attack from the enemy. Numerous new enemy earthworks were visible from the plain, however, indicating that the Confederates were planning to stay on the defensive.[16] The firing died down in the early afternoon without an attack being launched, and Franklin could breathe easier so far as the safety of his lines was concerned.

On General Sickles' division front, an arrangement was concluded between the opposing pickets for a mutual cease-fire. After this had been ratified by the Confederate division commander, the unofficial truce began, not to be broken during the remainder of the battle. This cease-fire allowed Sickles' medical aid men to recover some of Gibbon's wounded who had been lying within the Rebel picket line since the repulse on Saturday.[17]

In the Confederate camp, the cessation of hostilities on the thirteenth was assumed to be only temporary. General Lee telegraphed a message that night to Secretary of War James A. Seddon in which he indicated his expectation of a renewal of the attack at daylight.[18] The Union attacks had been quite persistent and, so far as the Confederates could determine, only a small portion of the enemy forces had been engaged. Therefore, this assumption was based on a sound military estimate. The capture of Burnside's order merely confirmed their belief that a dawn assault was being prepared. The only adjustments made in the Rebel dispositions was the relief of front-line units by reserves who had not seen action during the day. The accuracy and volume of the Federal fire directed at the stone wall position led to considerable entrenching during the hours of darkness, particularly on the crest of Marye's and Willis Hills. General Longstreet remained confident that his defense could hold, regardless of how many regiments were thrown against it.[19] On Jackson's front, A. P. Hill's battered division was moved back into reserve and replaced by the divisions of Early and Taliaferro.[20] Entrenchments were thrown up along this front since the Federal artillery had impressed on officers and men alike the value of field protection. Trees were felled and, particularly along the railroad winding in front of Jackson's right, barricades were erected.

When the sun dissipated the fog on Sunday morning, the Confederates from their vantage point on Marye's Hill could see for the first time the complete results of their determined defense of the day before. The many hundreds of dead and wounded lost in the assaults on the stone wall still lay where they had fallen. One of J.E.B. Stuart's cavalry officers, invited by an acquaintance to see that part of the battlefield, described the scene as follows:

> I saw it the day after the fight, and from the heights it looked as blue as if it had been covered with a blue cloth. At no one spot during our war were there as many bodies on the same space as here.[21]

Down at the stone wall, the defenders could hear the plaintive cry of the wounded calling for help and pleading for water. The mutual fear of a possible attack kept the rifles spitting at any man who moved into view on either side. Federal hospital attendants were turned back by rifle fire when they attempted to remove the wounded from the firing line or from the area between the lines. In one case, however, a Confederate soldier made an effort to relieve the suffering of the wounded Federals. Sergeant Richard Kirkland of Company E, Second South Carolina Volunteers, after listening to the low complaints of the wounded, secured permission from his commanding general to cross the wall to their aid. After first gathering several filled canteens, he went down to the wall on his errand of mercy. Since the Federal sharpshooters were quick to fire at any movement in the Rebel position, the sergeant decided to vault over the wall into full view, hoping this action would assure the enemy that his mission was a peaceful one. Fortunately, the Federals held their fire and for several hours during the afternoon he made many trips back to the wall to refill his canteens and dispense the contents to the injured men. Finally, after giving aid to all the wounded in his area, he returned to his unit and again took up his rifle.[22]

Following Burnside's acquiescence in the wishes of his subordinates not to order a new assault, a council of war was held at his headquarters. His scheme for a continued offensive effort overruled, he had to determine a new plan and do so quickly, before Lee had a chance to take advantage of the situation. The only sizeable units of his army which were not already committed were two of his cavalry brigades. Brigadier General William W. Averell's brigade, which was attached to the Center Grand Division, was still massed on Stafford Heights awaiting orders to cross. These troopers had bivouacked in the assembly areas they had occupied the night before the crossing began, when the crowded condition of Fredericksburg precluded their immediate employment.[23] A few men of the brigade had been used as flank guards upstream from Fredericksburg on the thirteenth, but the unit as a whole had not been employed. The brigade of cavalry attached to Sumner's Grand Division under Brigadier General Alfred Pleasonton was also waiting on the east bank of the river with the mission of protecting the exits of the upper bridges. Small units from this brigade had also been used to picket the right flank of the army, but no really serious work had been performed.[24] These two units contained only 6,294 cavalrymen and could hardy tip the scales in Burnside's favor at this late time. Earlier, they could have been of great value if employed as Stuart had used his men, but at this point in the operation it was too late to put them to work effectively.

The reserve support which Burnside really needed rested at the moment in the Eleventh and Twelfth Army Corps, under Major General Franz Sigel and Major General Henry W. Slocum, respectively. Together these two corps contained over 33,000 men, but they were not within supporting distance of Burnside's main army.[25] Orders had been sent rather belatedly to both units to move to Fredericksburg and support Burnside, but the orders were too late for effective compliance. They were not issued until the thirteenth, and at that time Sigel was in Dumfries and Slocum was still at Fairfax Courthouse, both places beyond the range of immediate support.[26]

With no significant reserve under his immediate control, Burnside was forced to depend on the troops actually on the field. With further attacks ruled out, the only decision left was to hold what had been won or to withdraw. Burnside's chief subordinates advocated a withdrawal of the main forces, but a retention of the Fredericksburg bridgehead which had been gained at such cost. In addition to the advantage the town presented as a bridgehead, they believed it would also salve Northern pride to save something from the week's operations. Burnside adopted this scheme so far as holding the town was concerned and issued orders to Hooker to place the city in a state of defense.[27] While these steps were being taken, the Commanding General pondered his next move, which inevitably involved a withdrawal since he had definitely decided against further offensive operations. Burnside seemed reluctant to take the logical step that decision had made imperative. While he procrastinated, the army quietly waited on the defensive for further orders.

In Washington, the civilian authorities waited anxiously for details of the fighting which had been so sparsely reported by Burnside on Saturday evening. The brief official dispatches allowed to get through for the benefit of the press merely indicated that fighting was in progress, but gave little idea of how well the Union arms were faring. In the absence of definite reports, rumors began to spread throughout the city concerning a bloody defeat at Fredericksburg. Secretary of of the Navy Gideon Welles, after a visit to the War Department, noted in his diary the possible truth of these rumors:

> The rumor at the War Department — and I get only rumor — is that our troops have done well, that Burnside and our generals are in good spirits; but there is something unsatisfactory, or not entirely satisfactory, in this intelligence, or in the method of communicating it. When I get nothing clear and explicit at the War Department I have my apprehensions. They fear to admit disastrous truths. Adverse tidings are suppressed, with a deal of fuss and mystery, a shuffling over of papers and maps, and a far-reaching vacant gaze at something undefined and indescribable.[28]

President Lincoln got his first eyewitness account from Henry Villard, a war correspondent for the New York *Tribune*. Villard had been with the army and sat up most of the night after the battle composing his account. Burnside, however, placed a news blackout on the reporters, refusing to pass their dispatches or allow them to leave the area. Villard managed to slip away from Aquia Landing just ahead of the Provost Marshal and was, therefore, the only reporter to get his story out. He contacted Senator Henry Wilson, and the Senator took him to the White House to tell his story to the President.

Villard had been appalled at the losses piled up in front of the stone wall and painted a rather dark picture of the plight of the Army of the Potomac. Lincoln listened to him intently and then, after thanking him for his report, added that he hoped the situation was not as bad as the reporter had indicated.[29] Although the President appeared confident when Villard had his interview, he was apparently somewhat uneasy, because he later tried to persuade General Halleck to order Burnside to withdraw the army across the river. Halleck characteristically declined to do this on the military grounds that it was always dangerous to interfere with field operations from a distance, the general on the ground being a better judge of what steps are necessary to safeguard his command.[30] Halleck's advice was accepted, and the next day a message expressing confidence in Burnside's ability to extricate the army was telegraphed to him by the General-in-Chief.[31]

Although Burnside appeared to agree with his council of war held on December 14, he did not issue any immediate orders to implement its decision. The army remained on the defensive throughout the remainder of Sunday. Meanwhile, some minor changes in position were made. As soon as night fell, the troops of Sykes's Division, were relieved. This relief made a considerable reduction in the strength of the front line. It was reduced to a strong picket line, and the men could now take better advantage of the available cover.[32] Except for the picket line, the main defense along the Fredericksburg sector now ran along the canal bluff. Similar adjustments were made all along the battle front, so that fresh troops were on the front line when the sun rose on Monday morning. The only activity occurring on Sumner's portion of the line consisted of desultory skirmishing between the pickets. The Confederates opened a new battery that had been emplaced during the night, enfilading some of the depressions the Union men were using for shelter and thereby causing some dislocation of the picket line. This battery also silenced with one direct hit the sharpshooters sheltered in the brick tannery.[33] Other than this brief flurry of activity, the front was quiet.

On the Federal left, little except the sporadic fire of pickets broke the quiet of the day. In the afternoon, a brief truce was arranged between Franklin and "Stonewall" Jackson so that the Federal wounded still lying within the Rebel lines could be recovered. During this cessation of hostilities, the men of both armies mingled in a friendly manner, exchanging tobacco and newspapers as if they had always been friends. When the last Federal wounded were carried back to their own lines, the truce was terminated, and the pickets took up their rifles and resumed their sniping as if the truce had never taken place.[34]

By noon on Monday, Burnside's order for the establishment of the city's defenses had filtered down to the corps level. General Couch was responsible for the defense of the city from Hanover Street left to the river, and Butterfield for the section from Hanover Street right to the river. To assist Butterfield in his defense, Whipple's Division was attached to the Fifth Corps for the remainder of the operation. The commanders involved were cautioned to keep the streets in the city clear for the rapid movement of reserves, particularly the streets leading to the bridges.[35]

Shortly after these orders were received by Couch and Butterfield, Burnside made an inspection trip to Fredericksburg to take another look at the situation firsthand. There was not much to see as far as enemy action was concerned, and certainly no indication of a Confederate attack in preparation. As the Commanding General crossed the bridge on his way back to headquarters, he was noticed by some men of the 118th Pennsylvania Volunteers, one of whom described his reception in these words: "There was always a kindly feeling for Burnside, but now his prescence stirred no enthusiasm; his appearance aroused no demonstration. It may have been a coincidence that, as he rode by, he drew his hat further down over his face."[36]

This second day of inaction was bringing Burnside to the point of no return. He either had to attack or withdraw, for Lee could not be expected to refrain from attacking forever, once he definitely determined that the Federals were not preparing a new assault. Painfully aware of this fact, Burnside, upon his return to the Phillips House, finally issued orders to his staff to begin preparations for a night withdrawal of the bulk of the army. The actual orders to the troop commanders were sent late that night.

Withdrawing the army across the river in the face of Lee's victorious forces was a ticklish proposition. If the Confederates discovered the movement before it was completed and launched an attack, a disaster might develop. Therefore, in order to maintain secrecy, a number of measures were taken to mufflle the sounds usually made by a large army on the move. Straw and earth were placed on the wooden pontoon bridges so that horses and wheeled vehicles could pass quietly over the river.[37] After dark, empty caissons were moved back and forth behind the picket lines causing the Confederates to think that new batteries were being moved into position.[38] The Union deception plan was carefully thought out and executed, thereby enabling this huge host to slip quietly across the river before Lee discovered the movement. During the last hours of the afternoon, the hospitals were cleared, and all the excess artillery was moved across the river in small groups so as not to arouse the Rebels' suspicions. The preparations were well underway when Franklin received the order at 6 p.m. to withdraw his wing of the army during the night. Immediately he telegraphed instructions to General Smith to begin the movement. Covered by a strong line of outposts, Franklin's men poured across the bridges and marched back to the same camps they had occupied before the battle had begun.[39]

General Couch was ordered to withdraw his command across the river at 10 p.m., leaving the defense of Fredericksburg to General Butterfield. Butterfield adjusted his units to cover that portion of the city exposed by Couch's withdrawal and continued his entrenching efforts, so that by dawn the city would be protected by a line of field fortifications along the outskirts of the town. This shift by Butterfield's Corps was completed without confusion. The Fifth Corps quietly assumed control of the Second Corps' sector as Couch's men withdrew.[40] Since the Confederate lines were so close to the Union positions at Fredericksburg, special precautions were taken to maintain the silence of the movement. Bayonet scabbards were removed and carried in the packs so they would not rattle against the canteens, and large fires were kept burning all along the line to simulate nighttime activities. Aiding the deception measures was a providential rainstorm which started about the same time as the first movement of troops. A strong wind was blowing from the Rebel lines toward the Union positions, and what few noises were made were not heard by the Confederate pickets.[41] A Confederate scout, ordered to determine if the Yankees were withdrawing, attempted to penetrate the picket line early in the evening and reported on his return: "I came near a closely deployed picket line; saw no opportunity of slipping through; could hear nothing to the front as the wind was blowing near a gale, so I returned."[42] The withdrawal continued in quite an orderly manner until 3:30 a.m. when, with Couch's troops safely across the river, Burnside ordered Butterfield to give up the city and withdraw also.

Thus, step by step, the Union army abandoned every gain it had made. Burnside was forced to the obvious conclusion that, unless there were immediate prospects for a new advance, the great risks involved in trying to hold the city with a small force would not be worth the price of a failure. The remaining divisions were covered during their retirement by the First Brigade of Sykes's Division, which was the last unit to cross at about 8 a.m. The bridges were then taken up one by one until only the bridges for the rear guard were left. The last connection with Fredericksburg was finally broken at 9 a.m., although some small parties of stragglers were later ferried over in pontoon boats manned by the engineers.[43] The entire operation was carried off with the skill of veteran troops, proving that the Army of the Potomac was still a smooth-functioning machine despite its recent setback.

As the sun dissipated the fog on the morning of December 16, the amazed Confederates found the vast plain, which the night before had been teeming with Federals, now completely empty. The picket line was pushed forward to the river, in the process of which small numbers of Union stragglers were captured, including an entire regimental band.[44] Many of the Confederate officers, including General Lee, had a fleeting suspicion that the Federals might decamp during the night. The possibility certainly existed for a decisive Confederate victory if Lee had acted on that premise. If Lee had launched a strong attack at dawn on December 14, he might have destroyed at least the Union right wing. As it was, the South had to be content with a Bunker Hill instead of a Cannae. Lee, in a letter to his wife written the same day as the Union withdrawal, indicated some of his chagrin at the final outcome of the Fredericksburg operations:

> Yesterday evening I had my suspicions that they might return during the night, but could not believe they would relinquish their hopes after all their boasting and preparation, and when I say that the latter is equal to the former you will have some idea of the magnitude. This morning they were all safe on the North side of the Rappahannock. They went as they came — in the night. They suffered heavily as far as the battle went, but it did not go far enough to satisfy me.[45]

Burnside, with his army now safely protected from the Confederates by the Rappahannock, saw his troops back in their bivouacs and then sat down to compose his report to Washington. While his dispatch was being readied, Union burial details crossed the river once more to bury the hundreds of dead still lying in front of the stone wall.[46] This depressing work completed, the last Federal soldier still west of the river returned to the main body on Stafford Heights. The reports of these parties completed the casualty lists, so that Burnside now knew the cost of his unsuccessful campaign. His loss totaled 1,281 killed; 9,477 wounded; and 1,769 missing — a grand total of 12,527 casualties. Of this number, 4,837 men were lost during Franklin's operations, and the rest fell in the assaults on the stone wall.

Blood is the coin of war, and the successful general spends it in quantity only when some important strategic or tactical advantage can be gained. But other than the loss inflicted on Lee, which totaled 4,756 men, Burnside had no advantage to report to his superiors.[47] On December 17, he dispatched his report in which he assumed the entire responsibility for the defeat: "For the failure in the attack I am responsible, as the extreme gallantry, courage, and endurance shown by the men was never excelled, and would have carried the points, had it been possible."[48] President Lincoln responded with a message to the men of the army in which he praised their bravery and sustained their general by pointing out, "Although you were not successful, the attempt was not an error, nor the failure other than accident."[49]

These brave words may have restored the morale of a few men in the Army of the Potomac, but thousands could see the Rebel rebuttal painted on a large sign erected on the Fredericksburg end of the railroad bridge. There, in large black letters, inspired by some unknown Confederate wag, the Yankees could read: "THIS WAY TO RICHMOND."

APPENDICES

APPENDIX A

Organization of the Union Forces
at the Battle of Fredericksburg, Va., December 11-15, 1862.[1]

ARMY OF THE POTOMAC
Maj. Gen. Ambrose E. Burnside

VOLUNTEER ENGINEER BRIGADE
Brig. Gen. Daniel P. Woodbury

ARTILLERY
Brig. Gen. Henry J. Hunt

RIGHT GRAND DIVISION
Maj. Gen. Edwin V. Sumner

SECOND ARMY CORPS
Maj. Gen. Darius N. Couch

FIRST DIVISION
Brig. Gen. Winfield S. Hancock

First Brigade
Brig. Gen. John C. Caldwell
Second Brigade
Brig. Gen. Thomas F. Meagher
Third Brigade
Col. Samuel K. Zook

SECOND DIVISION
Brig. Gen. Oliver O. Howard

First Brigade
Brig. Gen. Alfred Sully
Second Brigade
Col. Joshua T. Owen
Third Brigade
Col. Norman J. Hall

THIRD DIVISION
Brig. Gen. William H. French

First Brigade
Brig. Gen. Nathan Kimball
Second Brigade
Col. Oliver H. Palmer
Third Brigade
Col. John W. Andrews

NINTH ARMY CORPS
Brig. Gen. Orlando B. Willcox

FIRST DIVISION
Brig. Gen. William W. Burns

First Brigade
Col. Orlando M. Poe
Second Brigade
Col. Benjamin C. Christ
Third Brigade
Col. Daniel Leasure

SECOND DIVISION
Brig. Gen. Samuel D. Sturgis

First Brigade
Brig. Gen. James Nagle
Second Brigade
Brig. Gen. Edward Ferrero

THIRD DIVISION
Brig. Gen. George W. Getty

First Brigade
Col. Rush C. Hawkins
Second Brigade
Col. Edward Harland

CAVALRY DIVISION
Brig. Gen. Alfred Pleasonton

CENTER GRAND DIVISION
Maj. Gen. Joseph Hooker

THIRD ARMY CORPS
Brig. Gen. George Stoneman

FIRST DIVISION
Brig. Gen. David B. Birney

First Brigade
Brig. Gen. John C. Robinson
Second Brigade
Brig. Gen. J. H. Hobart Ward
Third Brigade
Brig. Gen. Hiram G. Berry

SECOND DIVISION
Brig. Gen. Daniel E. Sickles

First Brigade
Brig. Gen. Joseph B. Carr
Second Brigade
Col. George B. Hall
Third Brigade
Brig. Gen. Joseph W. Revere

THIRD DIVISION
Brig. Gen. Amiel W. Whipple

First Brigade
Brig. Gen. A. Sanders Piatt
Second Brigade
Col. Samuel S. Carroll

FIFTH ARMY CORPS
Brig. Gen. Daniel Butterfield

FIRST DIVISION
Brig. Gen. Charles Griffin

SECOND DIVISION
Brig. Gen. George Sykes

First Brigade
Col. James Barnes

First Brigade
Lt. Col. Robert C. Buchanan

Second Brigade
Col. Jacob B. Sweitzer

Second Brigade
Maj. George L. Andrews

Third Brigade
Col. T. B. W. Stockton

Third Brigade
Brig. Gen. G. K. Warren

THIRD DIVISION
Brig. Gen. Andrew A. Humphreys

First Brigade
Brig. Gen. Erastus B. Tyler

Second Brigade
Col. Peter H. Allabach

CAVALRY BRIGADE
Brig. Gen. William W. Averell

LEFT GRAND DIVISION
Maj. Gen. William B. Franklin

FIRST ARMY CORPS
Maj. Gen. John F. Reynolds

FIRST DIVISION
Brig. Gen. Abner Doubleday

SECOND DIVISION
Brig. Gen. John Gibbon

First Brigade
Col. Walter Phelps, Jr.

First Brigade
Col. Adrian Root

Second Brigade
Col. James Gavin

Second Brigade
Col. Peter Lyle

Third Brigade
Col. William F. Rogers

Third Brigade
Brig. Gen. Nelson Taylor

Fourth Brigade
Brig. Gen. Solomon Meredith

THIRD DIVISION
Maj. Gen. George G. Meade

First Brigade
Col. William Sinclair

Second Brigade
Col. Albert L. Magilton

Third Brigade
Brig. Gen. C. Feger Jackson

SIXTH ARMY CORPS
Maj. Gen. William F. Smith

FIRST DIVISION
Brig. Gen. William T. H. Brooks

First Brigade
Col. Alfred T. A. Torbert
Second Brigade
Col. Henry L. Cake
Third Brigade
Brig. Gen. David A. Russell

SECOND DIVISION
Brig. Gen. Albion P. Howe

First Brigade
Brig. Gen. Calvin E. Pratt
Second Brigade
Col. Henry Whiting
Third Brigade
Brig. Gen. Francis L. Vinton

THIRD DIVISION
Brig. Gen. John Newton

First Brigade
Brig. Gen. John Cochrane

Second Brigade
Brig. Gen. Charles Devens, Jr.

Third Brigade
Col. Thomas A. Rowley

CAVALRY BRIGADE
Brig. Gen. George D. Bayard

Organization of the Confederate Forces
at the Battle of Fredericksburg, Va., December 11-15, 1862.[2]

ARMY OF NORTHERN VIRGINIA
Gen. Robert E. Lee

FIRST CORPS
Lt. Gen. James Longstreet

McLAWS' DIVISION
Maj. Gen. Lafayette McLaws

Kershaw's Brigade
Brig. Gen. Joseph B. Kershaw
Barksdale's Brigade
Brig. Gen. William Barksdale
Semmes's Brigade
Brig. Gen. Paul J. Semmes
Cobb's Brigade
Brig. Gen. T. R. R. Cobb

HOOD'S DIVISION
Maj. Gen. John B. Hood

Law's Brigade
Brig. Gen. E. M. Law
Anderson's Brigade
Brig. Gen. George T. Anderson
Robertson's Brigade
Brig. Gen. J. B. Robertson
Toombs's Brigade
Col. H. L. Benning

PICKETT'S DIVISION
Maj. Gen. George E. Pickett

Garnett's Brigade
Brig. Gen. Richard B. Garnett
Kemper's Brigade
Brig. Gen. James L. Kemper
Armistead's Brigade
Brig. Gen. Lewis A. Armistead
Jenkins' Brigade
Brig. Gen. M. Jenkins
Corse's Brigade
Brig. Gen. Montgomery D. Corse

ANDERSON'S DIVISION
Maj. Gen. Richard H. Anderson

Wilcox's Brigade
Brig. Gen. Cadmus M. Wilcox
Featherston's Brigade
Brig. Gen. W. S. Featherston
Mahone's Brigade
Brig. Gen. William Mahone
Wright's Brigade
Brig. Gen. A. R. Wright
Perry's Brigade
Brig. Gen. E. A. Perry

RANSOM'S DIVISION
Brig. Gen. Robert Ransom, Jr.

Ransom's Brigade
Brig. Gen. Robert Ransom, Jr.
Cooke's Brigade
Brig. Gen. J. R. Cooke

SECOND CORPS
Lt. Gen. Thomas J. Jackson

D. H. HILL'S DIVISION
Maj. Gen. Daniel H. Hill

First Brigade
Brig. Gen. R. E. Rodes
Second (Ripley's) Brigade
Brig. Gen. George Doles
Third Brigade
Brig. Gen. A. H. Colquitt
Fourth Brigade
Brig. Gen. Alfred Iverson
Fifth (Ramseur's) Brigade
Col. Bryan Grimes

A. P. HILL'S DIVISION
Maj. Gen. Ambrose P. Hill

First (Field's) Brigade
Col. J. M. Brockenbrough
Second Brigade
Brig. Gen. Maxcy Gregg
Third Brigade
Brig. Gen. E. L. Thomas
Fourth Brigade
Brig. Gen. J. H. Lane
Fifth Brigade
Brig. Gen. J. J. Archer
Sixth Brigade
Brig. Gen. William D. Pender

119

EWELL'S DIVISION
Brig. Gen. Jubal A. Early

Lawton's Brigade
Col. E. N. Atkinson
Trimble's Brigade
Col. R. F. Hoke
Early's Brigade
Col. J. A. Walker
Hays' (First Louisiana) Brigade
Brig. Gen. Harry T. Hays

JACKSON'S DIVISION
Brig. Gen. Wm. B. Taliaferro

First Brigade
Brig. Gen. E. F. Paxton
Second Brigade
Brig. Gen. J. R. Jones
Third (Taliaferro's) Brigade
Col. E. T. H. Warren
Fourth (Starke's) Brigade
Col. Edmund Pendleton

RESERVE ARTILLERY
Brig. Gen. W. N. Pendleton

CAVALRY
Maj. Gen. James E. B. Stuart

FIRST BRIGADE
Brig. Gen. Wade Hampton
THIRD BRIGADE
Brig. Gen. W. H. F. Lee

SECOND BRIGADE
Brig. Gen. Fitzhugh Lee
ARTILLERY
Maj. John Pelham

APPENDIX B

Recapitulation of Losses for the Army of the Potomac,
December 11-15, 1862[1]

Unit	Killed	Wounded	Captured or Missing	Total Casualties
VOLUNTEER ENGINEER BRIGADE Brig. Gen. Woodbury	8	49	2	59
RIGHT GRAND DIVISION				
SECOND ARMY CORPS Maj. Gen. Couch				
FIRST DIVISION Brig. Gen. Hancock	219	1,584	229	2,032
SECOND DIVISION Brig. Gen. Howard	104	718	92	914
THIRD DIVISION Brig. Gen. French	89	904	167	1,160
NINTH ARMY CORPS Brig. Gen. Willcox				
FIRST DIVISION Brig. Gen. Burns	1	24	2	27
SECOND DIVISION Brig. Gen. Sturgis	94	827	86	1,007
THIRD DIVISION Brig. Gen. Getty	16	216	64	296
CENTER GRAND DIVISION				
THIRD ARMY CORPS Brig. Gen. Stoneman				
FIRST DIVISION Brig. Gen. Birney	114	655	181	950
SECOND DIVISION Brig. Gen. Sickles	12	85	3	100

Unit	Killed	Wounded	Captured or Missing	Total Casualties
THIRD DIVISION Brig. Gen. Whipple	19	92	18	129
FIFTH ARMY CORPS Brig. Gen. Butterfield				
FIRST DIVISION Brig. Gen. Griffin	73	733	120	926
SECOND DIVISION Brig. Gen. Sykes	17	163	48	228
THIRD DIVISION Brig. Gen. Humphreys	115	772	132	1,019
LEFT GRAND DIVISION				
FIRST ARMY CORPS Maj. Gen. Reynolds				
FIRST DIVISION Brig. Gen. Doubleday	31	161	22	214
SECOND DIVISION Brig. Gen. Gibbon	141	924	102	1,167
THIRD DIVISION Maj. Gen. Meade	175	1,241	437	1,853
SIXTH ARMY CORPS Maj. Gen. Smith				
FIRST DIVISION Brig. Gen. Brooks	24	123	50	197
SECOND DIVISION Brig. Gen. Howe	22	159	5	186
THIRD DIVISION Brig. Gen. Newton	7	47	9	63
Grand Total, Army of the Potomac	1,281	9,477	1,769	12,527

Recapitulation of Losses for the Army of Northern Virginia, December 11-15, 1862[2]

Unit	Killed	Wounded	Captured or Missing[3]	Total Casualties
FIRST CORPS				
Lt. Gen. Longstreet				
ANDERSON'S DIVISION	16	87	44	147
Maj. Gen. Anderson				
PICKETT'S DIVISION		46	1	47
Maj. Gen. Pickett				
RANSOM'S DIVISION	45	463		508
Brig. Gen. Ransom				
HOOD'S DIVISION	49	294	11	354
Maj. Gen. Hood				
McLAWS' DIVISION	17	464	66	547
Maj. Gen. McLaws				
WASHINGTON ARTILLERY	4	34		38
Col. J. B. Walton				
STUART'S CAVALRY		13		13
Maj. Gen. Stuart				
SECOND CORPS				
Lt. Gen. Jackson				
A. P. HILL'S DIVISION	211	1,408	417	2,036
Maj. Gen. Hill				
D. H. HILL'S DIVISION	26	146		172
Maj. Gen. Hill				
EWELL'S DIVISION	86	633	1	720
Brig. Gen. Early				
JACKSON'S DIVISION	5	167	2	174
Brig. Gen. Taliaferro				
Grand Total, Army of Northern Virginia	459	3,755	542	4,756

APPENDIX C

Tactical Study

The completion of the withdrawal of the Army of the Potomac brought to a close the operations which had culminated in the Battle of Fredericksburg. It was obvious to the lowest private, as it was to the civilians at home, that Burnside had suffered a complete defeat. His troops had been bloodily repulsed, and Lee in full strength was sitting squarely between the Federals and the road to Richmond. Strategically and tactically, Burnside had met his master. How had this result occurred? The Union army was larger and better equipped; it had fought as bravely as any fighting men ever had but to no avail. A brief military critique of the operations will reveal the reasons for Burnside's failure.

The reorganization of the Union army into three grand divisions at the beginning of the campaign proved to be unfavorable. In effect, Burnside had divided his army into three large combat teams. Each of these units was a combined arms team, which made it tactically self-sufficient once it was on the field of battle. The grand divisions, however, were unwieldy because of their size, since almost one-third of the entire army was in each unit. The basic fighting element which the army commander was most interested in maneuvering was the infantry division; but unless he usurped the authority of his grand division commander, he had to move six divisions at a time by maneuvering a complete grand division. Once in the presence of the enemy, Burnside found that he had to break up Hooker's Grand Division in order to provide support for the attacks by Sumner and Franklin. At the time Hooker was directed to attack with his grand division, his unit had been broken into nine separate parts. thus destroying its integrity and reducing the effective force under Hooker's direct control to less than an army corps.[1] As indicated, this organizational concept made it difficult to provide an adequate reserve without breaking up one of the grand divisions.

The assignment of the artillery and cavalry to each grand division led to the dispersal of these supporting troops throughout the army where in many cases they were not used efficiently. The assignment of batteries to the infantry divisions was useful in that each division commander was provided with field guns to use for the advancement and protection of his own command. However, Burnside could have better utilized some of these guns under central control. General Hunt had to withdraw divisional batteries for the protection of the river crossing and then return them to unit control for the battle. Many of these batteries, particularly on the right, were not engaged during the remainder of the action, while on the left every battery with Franklin was in the fight. The ten batteries which crossed the river with Sumner, only to be parked in the streets of Fredericksburg, could have been used to advantage by General Hunt. The dispersal of the cavalry proved even more wasteful since two of the brigades did not even cross the river and the third brigade, although it did cross, did not become engaged. If the cavalry had been kept under centralized control, the army commander would have been in a better position to commit them at the proper time and place.

The only type of operation for which the grand division organization was really suited was a campaign of swift movement on multiple axes.[2] Burnside did plan a campaign of movement — he hoped to sweep past Lee and win the foot race to Richmond — but, once this hope had been destroyed by various delays, Burnside should have readjusted his organization to provide a more flexible command. Inherent in the grand division command structure was an important weakness which contributed to the final failure. By placing one additional headquarters between the army commander and the basic maneuver elements, the army became less responsive to the will of the commander. In addition, the army commander became less aware of the actual combat situation, since he was primarily dealing with commanders who were acting as middlemen. If Burnside had kept himself better informed of the combat situation, this defect in organization might not have caused much trouble. But, with his lack of confidence, it tended to provide him with a means of insulating himself from the fighting units. Subconsciously he may have been trying to share with his grand division commanders the load of responsibility he carried. This may explain his failure to supervise the conduct of operations on December 13 more closely than he did. In any event, it would have been more effective to have retained the corps organization which existed in the Army of the Potomac when he took command.

Burnside's departure from the line of advance followed by Mc-Clellan to the Richmond, Fredericksburg, and Potomac R. R. revealed some merit, but the plan was impossible to execute due to logistical factors. His attempt to side-step Lee and gain a march on the road to Richmond presupposed that the Confederate capital was the primary objective of the Union forces. His selection of that city as the immediate objective of his operations was only a secondary step on the way to the really decisive objective of the conflict: the destruction of the Confederate army.

The Rebel army had been keeping out of reach of the Federals during the two-week movement from Berlin, Maryland, to Warrenton, Virginia, and it probably could have continued to do so. However, if Burnside had succeeded in skirting Lee and reaching Richmond, Lee would have had to unite his scattered forces and hasten to the defense of the capital. Then Burnside would have had the chance to destroy the main Confederate army and take the capital. The fact that this opportunity would have existed does not mean automatically that the Union commander would have succeeded. It does indicate that by making Richmond the immediate objective of his offensive movement, Burnside may have been taking the shortest road to reach his final objective.

Burnside's decision to cross the Rappahannock at Fredericksburg was a serious error. He could have crossed via the Rappahannock fords farther to the north and he would have placed his army in a position to take Fredericksburg by the flank. Instead, he chose to cross at a point where the river was unfordable. But the crossing was delayed, because the pontoons did not arrive on schedule. However, it should be pointed out that the plan to cross by bridges at Fredericksburg was submitted to General Halleck and President Lincoln, and although it did not arouse enthusiasm, it did receive approval. If this strategic move was not entirely acceptable to Burnside's superiors, they should have vetoed it at the time.

During the preliminary movements which vitally affected the outcome of the campaign, two fatal mistakes were made. The delay and failure of the bridge train to reach Falmouth in time to assist Sumner's Grand Division to cross as soon as it arrived was given by many officers as the chief reason for the defeat which followed. Franklin, when testifying before the Committee on the Conduct of the War which was in session at Falmouth on December 19, 1862, stated:

I would like to impress as firmly upon the committee as firmly as it is impressed upon my mind the fact that this whole disaster has resulted from the delay in the arrival of the pontoon bridges. Whoever is responsible for that delay is responsible for all the disasters which have followed.[3]

Although Franklin oversimplified the matter, his statement was, in the main, correct.

The actual delay of the trains was due to a series of unforeseen events, including a heavy rainstorm, compounded by General Halleck's lack of energy in supervision. The reason this delay proved fatal was Burnside's refusal to suspend the movement of his army for a few days. He knew the day before the troops left Warrenton that there had been a delay in forwarding the bridges, but he gambled that they would still arrive in time to be of use. His gamble failed, and the result was the end of his grand design to get around Lee's strategic right flank. Once the Union army moved in strength, Lee was certain to become aware of it and take countermeasures; but if Burnside had kept his forces inactive four or five days longer in the Warrenton concentration area, the Confederate commander would not have known what to expect.

Once the movement began, Burnside's three grand divisions made a commendably rapid march to Falmouth, leaving Lee temporarily uncertain of their objective. It was the day after Sumner had arrived at Falmouth that Lee sent Stuart toward Warrenton to find out Burnside's intentions. Lee could easily have been kept in the dark longer if the projected Union feint towards Culpeper had really been pushed vigorously. This feint was the main part of Burnside's deception plan and should have been executed with the same efficiency as the movement to Falmouth, but it was not. General Hooker, bringing up the rear of the army, simply covered the rear guard with cavalry instead of making a vigorous feint. If Hooker's Grand Division had been sent on the road to Culpeper on the same day that Sumner moved southeast toward Fredericksburg, it is quite possible that Lee would not have divined the Federal design for an additional two days. This movement would not have delayed Hooker's arrival at Falmouth, but it would have meant that his men would have been on the road four days instead of two. As it was, the feint was so weak that Stuart quickly penetrated the cavalry screen along the upper Rappahannock and discovered the direction of the Union move. Burnside was apparently so interested in his movement south that he failed to use sufficient deception to confuse the Confederate command.

When Sumner arrived opposite Fredericksburg on November 17, only a small picket force occupied the town and Lee's main army was still encamped, unaware that a forward movement had taken place. The bridges had not arrived. Sumner asked for permission to cross at once, since the enemy was not in force, but was ordered by Burnside to wait until the pontoons arrived. At this time troops could have been crossed, but the poor condition of the fords would have made it a slow operation and one that would have been difficult to support if the Rebels had reacted with large forces. Caution dictated that Sumner wait. But if Burnside had been bold and pushed across as many of Sumner's men as possible, they would have been in possession of the town and the heights before Lee received news of the movement. The Federal batteries on Stafford Heights would have reduced the chances of a swift thrust of large Rebel forces overwhelming the advance enemy force. If this force had acted boldly enough, Lee would have probably abandoned the Rappahannock country and fallen back to the North Anna River. It was not his intention to make a stand at Fredericksburg, and it was only the vacillation of the Federals that induced him to defend the line on the Rappahannock.[4]

After the pontoon trains arrived on November 25, two more weeks were wasted before the attempt to cross was made. Here again, delay only assisted the Rebels. Jackson did not receive the definite orders to join the main army until November 28, which means that Burnside, had he been ready to cross when the pontoons arrived, could have attacked Lee with one half of the Rebel army in position. The only possible reason for waiting was for the completion of logistical arrangements at Aquia Landing. But even if logistical facilities for the support of a push farther south were lacking, the opportunity to attack Lee before Jackson had had time to join him was too important to be overlooked. At Fredericksburg the Union and Confederate forces were so close together physically that Lee would have been obliged to fight at least a rear guard action before he could disengage. Burnside was unaware that the odds were in his favor.

The Fredericksburg crossing put the Federal troops in a tactical trap from which they could not extricate themselves, no matter how hard they fought. In this particular instance Burnside's reconnaissance efforts were incredibly meager. No use was made of cavalry units to penetrate the river barrier and find out what Rebel units were around Port Royal or Skinker's Neck; the observation balloon was not sent up until the day of the battle. The appearance of Confederate infantry at both points led Burnside to abandon efforts to cross the river below Lee's position, and apparently no thought was given to crossing above Falmouth and flanking the Rebels. The only reason advanced by Burnside for his choice of the Fredericksburg crossing site was that he believed the Rebel army to be divided, and that crossing would put the Union troops between the two parts of Lee's army. Thus the Confederate forces could be defeated piecemeal. How the sight of a few Rebel guns and men downriver could convince Burnside that Lee had really split his army in two is hard to understand, yet the Union commander's moves after crossing the river lead to the conclusion that he had expected to assault a divided enemy.[5]

The tactical details of the crossing as embodied in Burnside's orders left much to be desired and cost many Federal lives. Attempting to build bridges across a river when one bank is defended by a skillful enemy is the height of folly; yet none of the engineer officers or subordinate commanders pointed this out to their commanding general. Conceding that Burnside was ill-served by his subordinates in this matter, the weak operation order issued to the grand division commanders was inexcusable. It was sketchy in the extreme and, in effect, amounted to an order to cross the bridges and then be governed by circumstances. It is true that the situation to be faced after the river was crossed could not be completely anticipated but, with almost a month to plan, certainly a more definite order could have been devised. This lack of a positive order to his subordinates reveals the irresolute attitude of the commander-in-chief.

The crossing itself merely pointed up the inherent weaknesses of the tactical crossing plan. Barksdale's sharpshooters quickly demonstrated the futility of bridge-building in close proximity to trained riflemen. Despite the success of Hunt's artillery at the lower bridge sites, it should have been quickly apparent elsewhere that cannon fire alone could not suppress such Rebel defenders. Yet it was only after seven hours of repeated failures that the artillery commander, General Hunt, came up with the plan of crossing infantry first at the city bridge sites and then finishing the bridges. The relative ease with which this movement was made suggests that a similar one made earlier in the morning might have been just as successful.

Disregarding this delay, however, Burnside had it within his power to solve the problem at 9 a.m. that morning if he had chosen to do so.[6] Franklin was given orders to hold his troops in place until the bridges at the city were finished. For the rest of the day, therefore, his bridges stood idle while other Federal soldiers were shot down trying to build additional bridges one and one-half miles to the north. If Burnside had immediately crossed Franklin's Grand Division and sent a division into Fredericksburg from the south, Barksdale would have been flanked out of his position by noon. This movement would have been covered by the artillery on Stafford Heights along the entire route and would not have exposed Franklin to any serious risk. Here again, Burnside did not take advantage of the opportunities presented by the fortunes of battle. He stuck rigidly to the sketchy plan which had been issued the night before and threw away one more chance to hit Lee while part of his force was still watching the lower crossings.

The hard fighting of Burnside's assault units cleared Fredericksburg by nightfall; with the completion of the bridges, the crossing of the army could begin. Instead of rushing the army across that night and pushing on at dawn to dislodge Lee, Burnside waited until the next day to deploy over the bridges. The purpose of this suspension of movement on the night of December 11 was never explained by Burnside; and, although a surprise to his subordinates, it did not impress them as a possible cause for their defeat. The possibilities of success for the Union army if it had crossed on the night of December 11 and attacked the next morning are problematical, but it would certainly have faced a weaker defense. A night crossing of the army would have been difficult, but the same troops recrossed the river on the night of the withdrawal without incident, indicating the feasibility of such a movement. Two divisions of Jackson's Corps were still downriver and would not have been in supporting positions behind A. P. Hill's line if Meade could have made his attack on the morning of the twelfth.

The strange torpor affecting Burnside during the whole combat showed clearly in his attack order issued for the assault on the Confederate positions. The very wording of the order was vague and failed to explain the concept of the operation to the subordinates concerned. Probably this vagueness was chiefly due to the fact that Burnside himself was not exactly sure what he wanted to do. Couch indicated that Burnside's intentions kept changing after he got in the face of the enemy, which would explain the lack of definitiveness in the written orders.[7] After the battle, Burnside said that his plan was to seize the right flank of the Rebel position in order to sweep behind the Confederates and take them in flank and rear. If this was true, his orders did not give this impression. In fact, Franklin came to the conclusion that, instead of a major attack, Burnside was merely sending him on a reconnaissance-in-force.[8] The ambiguous wording of the order to Franklin, which included both a division attack on Prospect Hill and the movement of the main body down the Old Richmond Road, was contradictory and led Franklin to make the attack with insufficient numbers.

Barron Deaderick, in his *Strategy in the Civil War*, indicates that the attempt to attack Lee's position frontally showed Burnside's complete incompetence.[9] This criticism is generally accepted by military commentators, and yet it is not completely fair to the Union commander.[10] It is true that Lee could have been flanked out of his position by a wide turning movement, either above or below the position, and that this would have been preferable to crossing directly into Fredericksburg. Once Burnside had crossed, however, the only possible direction was straight ahead, short of giving up the campaign. The plan itself was quite faulty, in that the only hope for a frontal assault lay in making use of the Union superiority in numbers to overcome the Confederate army which was strung out along six miles of lines. But the obstructions back of Fredericksburg precluded attacks in mass, since only one or two brigades could attack at a time. However, on the left there was ample room for maneuver. It would have been much better, therefore, to have reduced Sumner's task to a feint and to have massed the rest of the army for a strong attack on Jackson's position. The plan which was followed resulted in weak attacks on both defense flanks, thereby dissipating the Union combat power.

Starting with this order, Burnside compounded the error by poor leadership techniques. The orders were not issued soon enough for his subordinates to interpret them and prepare the troops. Lack of understanding and preparation resulted in hasty and unsuccessful assaults. Burnside had ample time to conduct a briefing at headquarters and assure himself that his subordinates understood what he was trying to do. In Franklin's case, the commanding general did send a staff officer, General Hardie, to explain the contents of an order and prevent any possible misinterpretation. Evidently, Burnside continued to hope to catch Lee separated from Jackson and believed that a light tap against the front would send the Rebels fleeing. Two weeks before, when Jackson was still far away, Lee might have been routed. But after so much time had been wasted, the generals in the field knew that it was unrealistic to hope that anything but an all-out effort would produce results. Burnside was more and more out of touch with reality, as if he were operating in some sort of tactical vacuum.

The logistical details to support Burnside's attack were carefully and efficiently completed, and fighting troops were not in want of supplies during the battle. General Ingalls wrote the Quartermaster General in Washington that he was prepared to support instant forward movement of the army, and it is probable that he could have made good his claim.[11] During the entire Fredericksburg campaign only the operation conducted by grand division and subordinate headquarters showed military competence. Basically the Army of the Potomac was a sound, efficient army, but it was unsuccessful because it lacked direction from the top.

Franklin's execution of the attack order was later seized on as especially faulty, and he was made the scapegoat of the defeat by the Committee on the Conduct of the War. He was criticized for not employing more of his troops in the attack, so that Meade's initial gains could have been held and exploited. Meade's failure was simply one of lack of strength, the direct result of Burnside's order to attack with one division, well-supported. Franklin did use three divisions in the attack, and complied with both the letter and the spirit of Burnside's order, as he understood it. General Hardie was present while these movements were being planned; and if Franklin was not using the strength that Burnside had contemplated, Hardie should have made this fact known to the commander of the Right Grand Division. There is no indication that Franklin's commitment was short of that intended by Burnside.

Tactically, however, Franklin did make some mistakes which reduced the effectiveness of the assaults delivered by Meade and Gibbon. No reconnaissance was made prior to ordering Meade forward, and no protection was provided on the open left flank. The cavalry brigade, which Franklin kept under cover near the bridges, could have been used to advantage in screening Meade's flank and keeping Stuart's troopers from interfering with the deployment of the assault columns. Pelham could not have caused the confusion he did if the cavalry had first been used to clear the area on this open flank. The mobility of the cavalry could have been exploited here, leaving Doubleday's Division free to support the infantry assault.[12] The use of Doubleday as flank protection was not called for by the tactical situation existing on the left flank. Federal batteries on Stafford Heights were in position to fire into any major force attempting to attack Franklin's left. In addition, only light Confederate cavalry forces were operating in this area.

Franklin's failure to attack with his whole force, in compliance with Burnside's verbal order of the early afternoon, was cited by the Committee as an example of his lack of vigor. Arriving at the height of the confusion following the repulse of Meade and the subsequent Rebel pursuit, the order was given in the form of a wish of the commanding general, implying that Franklin could use his discretion in obeying it. A general forward movement of the Union line would not have had much chance of success, because at that moment it would have been uncoordinated, due to the disarray that Meade's repulse had caused in the Union line. Receiving the information that the right of the army was hard-pressed, Franklin was well within his rights as a subordinate commander to suspend a movement which he believed would fail and, in case of failure, might produce an even greater disaster. Longstreet pointed out after the war that Burnside's verbal order should have been more imperative if he desired the attack to be made regardless of the situation in Franklin's command. In his words, "Men bred as soldiers have no fancy for orders that carry want of faith on their face."[13] The defensive posture assumed by Franklin following the unsuccessful assault was excellent. His defense stopped Jackson's general attack at the end of the day before it got well underway. Much of the credit for this accomplishment belongs to the Federal artillery which served well during the entire battle. The accuracy and rapidity of the Union artillery fire received comment from most of the Confederate commanders engaged during the battle.

The failure of Franklin's attack was simply due to an assault force insufficient for the position to be taken. Meade indicated that if he had been supported by strong forces, his gains could have been held and exploited.[14] The accuracy of this statement is open to some question because of the strong reserves kept out of the fight by Jackson. Still, the immediate cause of Meade's repulse was a lack of numbers in the attacking column. Burnside's ambiguous order was responsible for the small size of the assaulting forces on his left, as has already been indicated. Thus the relatively minor tactical errors committed by Franklin did not cause the defeat at Fredericksburg; rather, the failure of the Left Grand Division was preordained by the commanding general's faulty plan of attack.

The conduct of the attack on the right by Sumner and Hooker was well-handled, considering the orders they received from their commanding general. Burnside, by ordering the Right Grand Division forward before Franklin had even delivered his attack, completely abandoned the plan of battle. Burnside indicated that the attack on the right was to be made *after* the enemy had been shaken by the loss of Prospect Hill and the establishment of Franklin on their flank. The only reason advanced by Burnside for the subsequent change was the need for haste which he felt took precedence over other considerations. In effect, Burnside was reduced to making a wild lunge against Marye's Heights, hoping that something might give way.

The tactical conduct of this phase of the operation was simple in that the obstacles between the city and the enemy position precluded anything other than a frontal assault on a narrow front. The initial plan of driving the enemy pickets into the stone wall position might have succeeded if it had been followed, but the slow deployment of the assaulting brigades led to failure. Because of the narrow front of attack, the Confederates were able to concentrate their firepower to such a degree that it was physically impossible to move across the soggy ground fast enough to get units up to the stone wall before they were shot to pieces. The failure of French's Division should have indicated early in the battle that bravery alone was not sufficient. From this point on, the repeated assaults contributed nothing to the success of the Union cause and only added to the casualty lists. During the course of the afternoon, sixteen separate assaults were made, each one of which was halted at least fifty yards from the final objective: The stone wall, which became a sort of bloody magnet for every Union brigade in the vicinity of Fredericksburg. After Couch had committed his entire corps without visible effect, Burnside compounded the folly by ordering Hooker into the same slaughterhouse.

Why Burnside did not suspend the attacks, after it had become obvious that they could not succeed, is hard to explain. It is understandable that Hooker failed to convince Burnside that the order to continue the assaults on the stone wall should be cancelled, because the two generals were not on friendly terms. Burnside made the same error on more than one battlefield. When his troops suffered a repulse, he would stubbornly keep on pounding away at that point until forced to quit. One of the newspaper correspondents with the army said of him:"Whenever he gets a positive order to GO, he will GO if it breaks his neck."[15] At Antietam, Burnside had sent unit after unit charging across the Burnside Bridge until finally the position was won, but the number of casualties was appalling. Later in the war, during the Battle of the Crater, he was to do the same thing by pushing troops into the crater long after there was any hope of success.

It was not that he was indifferent to loss of life, but he seemed to lose all tactical judgment when his men were repulsed. It is probably close to the truth to state that Burnside became so appalled at his heavy losses that he could not think clearly and therefore simply repeated his original orders. This perseverance would have been fine in a regimental commander who had only to follow orders literally, but the commanding general of an army has to be more flexible in order to take advantage of enemy weaknesses as they are revealed during the conduct of a battle.

When the last attacks were undertaken the large numbers of Union soldiers along the line of march seriously impeded the advance of the assaulting columns. These soldiers served no useful purpose and should have been withdrawn. If an attack had to be made, the best plan would have been to adopt a suggestion made by General Hooker to form a long column of assault and charge the stone wall under cover of darkness.[16] The dark uniforms of the Federals blending into the night would have assisted this movement.

The complete failure of the attack on Marye's Heights merely confirms Burnside's initial decision to attempt it only when the enemy was shaken and in the act of withdrawing. Of all the errors committed by Burnside during the battle, this one — ordering the premature assault by Sumner — had the most tragic consequences. The loss of life in front of the stone wall was the pathetic price paid for the commander's impatience and frustration.

The intention to renew the attack on the same line on Sunday morning was the decision of a man out of his senses. Fortunately his subordinates stepped in and, in effect, overruled him. Unable to find a single officer who would agree to further attacks on the stone wall, Burnside had to desist. The fact that no orders were issued to the grand divisions on Sunday and Monday indicates a lapse in direction from general headquarters after the shock of the defeat on Saturday had set in. The final decision to withdraw across the river was the only one open to Burnside, and the details which were completed by his subordinates showed intelligence and military skill. The one bright spot in the entire operation was this withdrawal which speaks volumes for the professional ability of the Army of the Potomac and makes the misdirection of the commanding general even more glaring.

These were the errors, from a military standpoint, which were committed during the Fredericksburg operations. The military men of the period learned several important lessons from the strategic and tactical details of the battle, details which were taken into account during the remainder of the war. Strategically, the failure to penetrate the Fredericksburg position led the Union command to favor the strategy of flanking it by crossing the fords on the upper Rappahannock. Burnside's grand division organization was abandoned for the more flexible corps organization, and the cavalry was organized under central control for similar reasons. The costly lesson taught the Federal engineers by Barksdale and his men was not lost on the Union commanders, and there were no further occasions in which bridges were constructed from a friendly to an enemy-held bank. The value of field entrenchments was impressed on both armies at Fredericksburg; and, during the remainder of the war, the spade became as important to the front-line soldier as the rifle. The tremendous effect of firepower employed against massed formations was amply proved in front of the stone wall, but this fact was not thoroughly appreciated and the lesson had to be repeated several times during the remainder of the conflict. The practical use of field wire communications and aerial observation was demonstrated at Fredericksburg, although neither became vital battlefield necessities until more recent years.

The failure of Burnside as an army commander was a tragedy in many ways. He did not have the qualifications required for the generalship of the Army of the Potomac. He was a slow thinker and he seemed unable to direct successfully an operation involving more than a few thousand men. He himself was aware of his shortcomings, and the responsibility of an entire army weighed heavily upon him. He was so fearful of making a mistake that it was almost impossible for him to make the simplest decisions. Irresolute, yet knowing that he, in the end, had to issue the orders, Burnside alternately went from periods of inactivity to bursts of unfortunate activity. When his actions finally culminated in complete disaster, he gave way to remorse and self-condemnation.

General Burnside manfully took full responsibility for the disaster and was widely admired for his moral courage in doing so. Many citizens at the time felt that, although Burnside had shouldered the blame, there were others more responsible than he. The private soldiers were not swayed by partisan political views, however, and showed no inclination to whitewash the commanding general. They realized that he had sent them on a mission that no amount of bravery and sacrifice of life could accomplish. One soldier, in a letter home, expressed the feelings of his comrades:

"You say that I don't say how we all take our defeat. We take that whipping like a parcel of schoolboys would take a whipping. . . . One boy blames the other for getting them all whipped, and finally [they] come to the conclusion that if it wasn't for the master none of them would have got it."[17]

A dispassionate study of the facts reveals no need to temper that soldier's simple verdict.

BIBLIOGRAPHY

BIBLIOGRAPHIES

Beers, Henry P. *Bibliographies in American History.* New York: The H. W. Wilson Company, 1942.

Dutcher, George M., *et al. Guide to Historical Literature.* New York: The Macmillan Company, 1931.

Handlin, Oscar, *et al. Harvard Guide to American History.* Cambridge, Mass.: The Belknap Press, 1955.

Index to the Writings on American History, 1902-1940. Washington, D. C.: American Historical Association, 1956.

Larned, J. N. *The Literature of American History.* Boston: Houghton Mifflin Company, 1902.

U. S. Government, Department of the Army. *The Writing of American Military History: A Guide,* Department of the Army Pamphlet No. 20-200. Washington, D. C.: U. S. Government Printing Office, 1956.

GENERAL WORKS

Adams, George W. *Doctors in Blue.* New York: Henry Schuman, 1952.

Beardslee Magneto-Electric Company. *Beardslee's Military Telegraph.* New York: John A. Gray and Green, Printers, 1863.

Brockett, Linus P. *Women's Work in the Civil War.* Philadelphia: Zeigler McCurdy and Company, 1867.

Brown, J. Willard. *The Signal Corps, U. S. A.* Boston: B. Wilkins and Company, 1896.

Buchanan, Lamont. *A Pictorial History of the Confederacy.* New York: Crown Publishers, 1951.

Casey, Brig. Gen. Silas. *Infantry Tactics.* 3 vols. New York: D. Van Nostrand, 1862.

Croffut, William A. *The Military and Civil History of Connecticut.* New York: Ledyard Bill, 1869.

Davis, Jefferson. *The Rise and Fall of the Confederate Government.* Vol. II. New York: D. Appleton and Company, 1912.

Deaderick, Barron. *Strategy in the Civil War.* Harrisburg, Pa.: The Military Service Publishing Company, 1951.

Dupuy, R. Ernest, and Dupuy, Trevor N. *Military Heritage of America.* New York: McGraw-Hill Book Company, Inc., 1956.

Duyckinck, Evert A. *National History of the War for the Union, Civil, Military, and Naval.* Vol. III. New York: Johnson, Fry and Company, 1865.

Eggleston, George C. *The History of The Confederate War.* Vol. II. New York: Sturgis and Walton Company, 1910.

Elson, Henry W. *The Civil War Through the Camera.* New York: Trow Directory Printing and Bookbinding Company, 1912.

Fox, William F. *Regimental Losses in the American Civil War 1861-1865.* Albany, N. Y.: Albany Publishing Company, 1889.

Goolrick, John T. *Historic Fredericksburg.* Richmond, Va.: Whittet and Shepperson, 1922.

Greeley, Horace. *The American Conflict.* Vol. II. Hartford, Conn.: O. D. Case and Company, 1866.

Hardee, Lt. Col. W. J. *Rifle and Light Infantry Tactics.* 2 vols. Philadelphia: J. B. Lippincott and Company, 1861.

Haydon, F. Stansbury. *Aeronautics in the Union and Confederate Armies.* Vol. I. Baltimore: The Johns Hopkins Press, 1941.

Headley, Joel Tyler. *The Great Rebellion.* Vol. II. Hartford, Conn.: American Publishing Company, 1866.

Hosmer, James Kendall. *The American Civil War.* Vol. I. New York: Harper and Brothers, 1913.

Lee, Guy Carleton. *The True History of the Civil War.* Philadelphia: J. B. Lippincott and Company, 1903.

Livermore, Thomas L. *Numbers and Losses in the Civil War.* Boston: Houghton Mifflin Company, 1901.

Lonn, Ella. *Foreigners in the Union Army and Navy.* Baton Rouge, La.: Louisiana State University Press, 1951.

Lossing, Benson J. *Pictorial History of the Civil War.* Vol. II. Hartford, Conn.: T. Belknap, 1868.

McMaster, John B. *A History of the People of the United States During Lincoln's Administration.* New York: D. Appleton and Company, 1927.

Miller, Francis T. (ed.). *The Photographic History of the Civil War.* Vol. II. New York: The Review of Reviews Company, 1911.

Mitchell, Joseph B. *Decisive Battles of the Civil War.* New York: G. P. Putnam's Sons, 1955.

Paris, Louis Philippe Albert D'Orleans. *History of the Civil War in America.* Vol. II. Philadelphia: Porter and Coates, 1875-88.

Pollard, Edward Albert. *Southern History of the War: The Second Year.* New York: Charles B. Richardson, 1864.

Quinn, Silvanus J. *The History of the City of Fredericksburg, Virginia.* Richmond, Va.: The Hermitage Press, 1908.

Randall, James G. *The Civil War and Reconstruction.* New York: D. C. Heath and Company, 1937.

Rhodes, James F. *History of the Civil War.* New York: The Macmillan Company, 1917.

Ropes, John Codman. *The Story of the Civil War.* Vol. II. New York: G. P. Putnam's Sons, 1933.

Sandburg, Carl. *Storm Over the Land.* New York: Harcourt, Brace and Company, 1942.

Shotwell, Walter Gaston. *The Civil War in America.* Vol. II. New York: Longmans, Green and Company, 1923.

Smith, Edward P. *Incidents of the United States Christian Commission.* Philadelphia: J. B. Lippincott and Company, 1869.

Starr, Louis Morris. *Bohemian Brigade.* New York: Alfred A. Knopf, 1954.

Victor, Orville J. *The History of the Southern Rebellion.* Vol. III. New York: James D. Torrey, 1868.

Weisberger, Bernard A. *Reporters for the Union.* Boston: Little, Brown and Company, 1953.

Wise, Jennings C. *The Long Arm of Lee.* Vol. I. Lynchburg, Va.: J. P. Bell Company, 1915.

BIOGRAPHIES

Barton, William E. *The Life of Clara Barton.* Vol. I. New York: Houghton Mifflin Company, 1922.

Cooke, John E. *Stonewall Jackson.* New York: D. Appleton and Company, 1866.

Dyer, John P. *The Gallant Hood.* Indianapolis, Ind.: The Bobbs-Merrill Company, Inc., [1950].

Eckenrode, Hamilton J. *George B. McClellan: The Man Who Saved the Union.* Chapel Hill, N. C.: The University of North Carolina Press, 1941.

Freeman, Douglas S. *Lee's Lieutenants.* Vol. II. New York: Charles Scribner's Sons, 1946.

Freeman, Douglas S. *R. E. Lee.* Vols. I and II. New York: Charles Scribner's Sons, 1935.

Fuller, John F. C. *Grant and Lee.* London: Eyre and Spottiswoode, 1933.

Hassler, Warren W., Jr. *General George B. McClellan: Shield of the Union.* Baton Rouge, La.: Louisiana State University Press, 1957.

Henderson, Lt. Col. George F. R. *Stonewall Jackson and the American Civil War.* Vol. II. New York: Longmans, Green and Company, 1900.

Johnson, Allen, and Malone, Dumas (eds.). *Dictionary of American Biography.* Vols. III, VI, XVIII, IX, and XI. New York: Charles Scribner's Sons, 1928-44.

Macartney, Clarence E. *Lincoln and His Generals.* Philadelphia: Dorrance and Company, 1925.

McClellan, Henry B. *The Life and Campaigns of Major-General J. E. B. Stuart.* New York: Houghton Mifflin Company, 1885.

Poore, Ben P. *Major General Ambrose Everett Burnside.* Providence, R. I.: J. A. and R. A. Reid and Company, 1882.

Sanger, Donald Bridgman. *James Longstreet, Soldier.* Baton Rouge, La.: Louisiana State University Press, 1952.

Thomason, John William, Jr. *JEB Stuart.* New York: Charles Scribner's Sons, 1953.

Williams, Kenneth P. *Lincoln Finds a General.* New York: The Macmillan Company, 1949.

Williams, Thomas H. *Lincoln and His Generals.* New York: Alfred A. Knopf, 1952.

Woodbury, Augustus. *Major General Ambrose E. Burnside and the Ninth Army Corps.* Providence, R. I.: Sidney S. Rider and Brother, 1867.

CAMPAIGN AND UNIT HISTORIES

Allan, William. *The Army of Northern Virginia in 1862.* Boston: Houghton Mifflin Company, 1892.

Bennett, Andrew J. *The Story of the First Massachusetts Light Battery.* Boston: Press of Deland and Barta, 1886.

Brewer, A. T. *History of the Sixty-first Regiment Pennsylvania Volunteers 1861-1865.* Pittsburgh: Art Engraving and Printing Company, 1911.

Bruce, George A. *The Twentieth Regiment of Massachusetts Volunteer Infantry 1861-1865.* New York: Houghton Mifflin Company, 1906.

Child, William. *A History of the Fifth Regiment New Hampshire Volunteers.* Bristol, N. H.: R. W. Musgrove, 1893.

Cogswell, Leander W. *A History of the Eleventh New Hampshire Regiment, Volunteer Infantry in the Rebellion War, 1861-1865.* Concord, N. H.: Republican Press Association, 1891.

Conyngham, David P. *The Irish Brigade and Its Campaigns.* New York: William McSorley and Company, 1867.

Cook, Benjamin F. *History of the Twelfth Massachusetts Volunteers.* Boston: Twelfth (Webster) Regiment Association, 1882.

Craft, David. *History of the One Hundred Forty-first Regiment Pennsylvania Volunteers 1862-1865.* Towanda, Pa.: Reporter-Journal Printing Co., 1885.

Cudworth, Warren Handel. *History of the First Regiment Massachusetts Infantry.* Boston: Walker, Fuller and Co., 1866.

Cuffel, Charles A. *History of Durell's Battery in the Civil War.* Philadelphia: Craig, Finley and Co., Printers, 1903.

Ewing, John, *et al. Under the Maltese Cross.* Pittsburgh: The 155th Regimental Association, 1910.

Gates, Theodore B. *The Ulster Guard and the War of the Rebellion.* New York: Benjamin H. Tyrrel, 1879.

Gould, Joseph. *The Story of the Forty-Eighth.* Philadelphia: Alfred M. Slocum Co., 1908.

Gracey, Samuel Lewis. *Annals of the Sixth Pennsylvania Cavalry.* Philadelphia: E. H. Butler and Co., 1868.

Graham, Matthew J. *The Ninth Regiment New York Volunteers (Hawkins' Zouaves).* New York: E. P. Coby and Co., 1900.

Hays, Gilbert Adams. *Under the Red Patch.* Pittsburgh: Sixty-third Pennsylvania Volunteers Regimental Association, 1908.

Henderson, Lt. Col. George F. R. *The Campaign of Fredericksburg.* 3d ed. London: Gale and Polden, Ltd., [1891].

Mark, Penrose G. *Red, White, and Blue Badge.* Harrisburg, Pa.: The Aughinbaugh Press, 1911.

McDermott, Anthony W. *A Brief History of the 69th Regiment Pennsylvania Veteran Volunteers.* Philadelphia: D. J. Gallagher and Co., 1889.

Mulholland, St. Clair A. *The Story of the 116th Regiment Pennsylvania Volunteers.* Philadelphia: F. McManus, Jr., and Co., Printers, 1903.

Palfrey, Brig. Gen. Francis Winthrop. *The Antietam and Fredericksburg.* New York: Charles Scribner's Sons, 1882.

Parker, Thomas H. *History of the 51st Regiment of P. V. and V. V.* Philadelphia: King and Baird, Printers, 1869.

Powell, William H. *The Fifth Army Corps, Army of the Potomac.* New York: G. P. Putnam's Sons, 1896.

Redway, G. W. *Fredericksburg.* London: George Allen and Unwin, Ltd., 1906.

Rowe, David W. *A Sketch of the 126th Regiment Pennsylvania Volunteers.* Chambersburg, Pa.: Cook and Hays, 1869.

Schalk, Emil. *Campaigns of 1862 and 1863.* Philadelphia: J. B. Lippincott and Co., 1863.

Stackpole, Edward J. *Drama on the Rappahannock: The Fredericksburg Campaign.* Harrisburg, Pa.: The Military Service Publishing Co., 1957.

Steele, Matthew Forney. *American Campaigns.* Washington, D. C.: United States Infantry Association, 1922.

Stine, James H. *History of the Army of the Potomac.* Philadelphia: Rodgers Printing Co., 1892.

Survivors' Association, 118th Pennsylvania Infantry Regiment, *Antietam to Appomattox.* Philadelphia: J. L. Smith, 1892.

Swinton, William. *Campaigns of the Army of the Potomac.* New York: Charles Scribner's Sons, 1882.

Sypher, Josiah R. *History of the Pennsylvania Reserve Corps.* Lancaster, Pa.: Elias Barr and Co., 1865.

Thomson, Osmond R. H., and Rauch, William. *History of the "Bucktails."* Philadelphia: Electric Printing Co., 1906.

Todd, William. *The Seventy-Ninth Highlanders New York Volun-*

teers in the War of the Rebellion. Albany: Press of Brandoro, Barton and Co., 1886.

Vautier, John D. *History of the 88th Pennsylvania Volunteers.* Philadelphia: J. B. Lippincott and Co., 1894.

Walker, Brig. Gen. Francis A. *History of the Second Corps in the Army of the Potomac.* New York: Charles Scribner's Sons, 1886.

Ward, Joseph R. C. *History of the 106th Regiment Pennsylvania Volunteers.* Philadelphia: F. McManus, Jr., and Co., 1906.

Weygant, Charles H. *History of the One Hundred and Twenty-Fourth Regiment N. Y. S. V.* Newburgh, N. Y.: Journal Printing House, 1877.

Weymouth, H. G. O., *et al. History of the Nineteenth Regiment Massachusetts Volunteer Infantry.* Salem, Mass.: The Salem Press Co., 1906.

Woodward, Evan M. *History of the Third Pennsylvania Reserve.* Trenton, N. J.: MacCrellish and Quigley, Printers, 1883.

Woodward, Evan M. *Our Campaigns.* Philadelphia: J. E. Potter, 1865.

MEMOIRS, DIARIES, AND REMINISCENCES

Alexander, E. Porter. *Military Memoirs of a Confederate.* New York: Charles Scribner's Sons, 1907.

Beatty, John. *Memoirs of a Volunteer.* New York: W. W. Norton and Co., 1946.

Bennett, Edwin C. *Musket and Sword, or the Camp, March, and Firing Line in the Army of the Potomac.* Boston: Coburn Publishing Co., 1900.

Blackford, William Willis. *War Years with Jeb Stuart.* New York: Charles Scribner's Sons, 1945.

Brinton, John H. *Personal Memoirs of John H. Brinton.* New York: The Neale Publishing Co., 1914.

Coffin, Charles C. *Four Years of Fighting.* Boston: Ticknor and Fields, 1866.

Cox, Jacob D. *Military Reminiscences of the Civil War.* New York: Charles Scribner's Sons, 1900.

Douglas, Henry K. *I Rode with Stonewall.* Chapel Hill, N. C.: The University of North Carolina Press, 1940.

Early, Jubal A. *Autobiographical Sketch and Narrative of the War Between the States.* Philadelphia: J. B. Lippincott Co., 1912.

Ellis, Edward S. *The Camp Fires of General Lee.* Philadelphia: Henry Harrison and Co., 1886.

Fletcher, William A. *Rebel Private Front and Rear.* Austin, Tex.: University of Texas Press, 1954.

Haupt, Herman. *Reminiscences of Herman Haupt.* Milwaukee, Wisconsin: Wright and Joys Co., 1901.

Hitchcock, Frederick L. *War from the Inside.* Philadelphia: J. B. Lippincott Co., 1904.

Holmes, Oliver Wendell, Jr. *Touched with Fire.* Cambridge, Mass.: Harvard University Press, 1946.

Hood, John Bell. *Advance and Retreat.* New Orleans: Published for Hood Orphan Memorial Fund, 1880.

Howard, Oliver Otis. *Autobiography of Oliver Otis Howard.* 2 vols. New York: The Baker and Taylor Co., 1907.

Jones, J. B. *A Rebel War Clerk's Diary.* Vol. I. New York: Old Hickory Bookshop, 1935.

Lee, Captain Robert E. *Recollections and Letters of General Robert E. Lee.* New York: Doubleday, Page and Co., 1909.

Long, Armistead L. *Memoirs of Robert E. Lee.* New York: J. M. Stoddart and Co., 1886.

Longstreet, James. *From Manassas to Appomattox.* 2d ed. Philadelphia: J. B. Lippincott Co., 1903.

McClellan, George B. *McClellan's Own Story.* New York: C. L. Webster and Co., 1887.

Meade, George G. *The Life and Letters of George Gordon Meade.* New York: Charles Scribner's Sons, 1913.

Pickett, George E. *Soldier of the South.* Boston: Houghton Mifflin Co., 1928.

Pogue, William T. *Gunner with Stonewall.* Jackson, Tenn.: Mc-Cowat-Mercer Press, Inc., 1957.

Shotwell, Randolph A. *The Papers of Randolph Abbott Shotwell.* Vol. I. Raleigh, N. C.: The North Carolina Historical Commission, 1929.

Small, Maj. Abner R. *The Road to Richmond.* Berkeley, Calif.: University of California Press, 1939.

Sorrel, G. Moxley. *Recollections of a Confederate Staff Officer.* 2d ed. New York: The Neale Publishing Company, 1917.

Stevens, George T. *Three Years in the Sixth Corps.* Albany, N. Y.: S. R. Gray, 1866.

Stiles, Robert. *Four Years Under Marse Robert.* New York: The Neale Publishing Co., 1903.

Strong, George T. *The Diary of George Templeton Strong: The Civil War.* New York: The Macmillan Co., 1952.

Taylor, Walter H. *Four Years with General Lee.* New York: D. Appleton and Co., 1878.

Trobriand, Maj.-Gen. Regis de. *Four Years with the Army of the Potomac.* Boston: Ticknor, 1889.

Von Borcke, Heros. *Memoirs of the Confederate War for Independence.* Vol. II. New York: Peter Smith, 1938.

Welles, Gideon. *Diary.* Vol. I. Boston: Houghton Mifflin Co., 1911.

Whitman, Walt. *The Wound Dresser.* New York: The Bodley Press, 1949.

COLLECTED LETTERS AND DOCUMENTS

Andrews, J. Cutler. *The North Reports the Civil War.* Pittsburgh: University of Pittsburgh Press, 1955.

The Annals of the War. Philadelphia: The Times Publishing Co., 1879.

Basler, Roy P. (ed.). *The Collected Works of Abraham Lincoln.* Vol. V. New Brunswick, N. J.: Rutgers University Press, 1953.

Blackford, Charles M. *Letters from Lee's Army.* New York: Charles Scribner's Sons, 1947.

Commager, Henry S. (ed.). *The Blue and the Gray.* Vol. I. Indianapolis: The Bobbs-Merrill Co., Inc., 1950.

Eisenschiml, Otto (ed.). *The American Iliad.* Indianapolis: The Bobbs-Merrill Co., Inc., 1947.

Johnson, Robert U., and Buel, Clarence C. (eds.). *Battles and Leaders of the Civil War.* Vol. III. New York: The Century Co., 1888.

Marx, Karl, and Engels, Frederick. *The Civil War in the United States.* Edited by Richard Enmale. New York: International Publishers, 1937.

Moore, Frank (ed.). *The Rebellion Record: A Diary of American Events.* Vol. VI. New York: G. P. Putnam, 1863.

GOVERNMENT DOCUMENTS

Board of Artillery Officers. *Instruction for Field Artillery.* Philadelphia: J. B. Lippincott and Co., 1861.

Board of Artillery Officers. *Instruction for Field Artillery.* Washington: Government Printing Office, 1864.

U. S. Congress, Joint Committee on the Conduct of the War. *Senate Reports, No. 108.* Vol. II. 37th Cong., 3d Sess., 1863.

U. S. Senate. *Journal of the Congress of the Confederate States of America 1861-1865.* Vol. III. 58th Cong., 2d Sess., 1904. Senate Document No. 234.

U. S. Surgeon-General's Office. *The Medical and Surgical History of the War of the Rebellion.* 2d Issue, 1875.

U. S. War Department. *The War of the Rebellion: A Compilation of the Official Records of the Union and Confederate Armies.* Series I, Volume XXI, 1888.

U. S. War Department. *Atlas to Accompany the Official Records of the Union and Confederate Armies.* 1891-1895.

PERIODICALS

Alexander, Lt. Col. E. Porter. "The Battle of Fredericksburg," *Papers, Southern Historical Society*, X (1878), 382-445.

Daily Pittsburgh Gazette and Commercial Journal. November, 1862-January, 1863.

Harper's Weekly (New York). November, 1862-January, 1863.

New York Daily Tribune. November, 1862-January, 1863.

New York Times. November, 1862-January, 1863.

Public Ledger (Philadelphia). November, 1862-January, 1863.

The Reporter and Tribune (Washington, Pa.). November, 1862-January, 1863.

OTHER SOURCES

Boston, William. "The Civil War Diary of William Boston." Ann Arbor, Michigan: Orlan W. Boston, 1937. (Ditto process.)

Gordon, Stephen. "The Diary of Stephen Gordon." Manuscript on file at the Fredericksburg and Spotsylvania National Military Park Museum, Fredericksburg, Virginia.

Map, *State Highway System*, Commonwealth of Virginia, Department of Highways, 1956.

McDonald, Major John W. "The Battle of Fredericksburg." Unpublished manuscript in possession of Fredericksburg and Spotsylvania National Military Park Museum, Fredericksburg, Virginia.

The National Atlas. Philadelphia: O. W. Gray and Son, 1878.

Spaulding, Branch. "The Battle of Fredericksburg." Typescript. On file as part of official records of the National Park Service at the Fredericksburg and Spotsylvania National Military Park Museum, Fredericksburg, Virginia.

NOTES

CHAPTER I

1. Thomas L. Livermore, *Numbers and Losses in the Civil War* (Boston: Houghton Mifflin Company, 1901), p. 96.
2. Organization of the Union forces at the battle of Fredericksburg, Va., December 11-15, 1862, *The War of the Rebellion: A Compilation of the Official Records of the Union and Confederate Armies* (Washington, D. C.: Government Printing Office, 1888), Series I, Volume XXI, pp. 48-61. Cited hereafter as *O. R.* Since all references are to Series I, Volume XXI, only the page numbers will be cited.
3. *Ibid.*
4. Report of Maj. Gen. Hooker, *O. R.,* p. 357.
5. Letter, Maj. Gen. Sigel to Lt. Col. Richmond, Assistant Adjutant General, November 18, 1862, and letter, Maj. Gen. Slocum to Maj. Gen. Halleck, November 30, 1862, *O. R.,* pp. 770 and 813.
6. Livermore, *Numbers and Losses in the Civil War,* p. 96.
7. Douglas S. Freeman, *Lee's Lieutenants* (New York: Charles Scribner's Sons, 1946), II, p. 248.
8. Organization of the Army of Northern Virginia, *O. R.,* pp. 538-44.
9. Jennings C. Wise, *The Long Arm of Lee* (Lynchburg, Virginia: J. P. Bell Company, 1915), I, pp. 284-86, 358-60.

CHAPTER II

1. Jacob D. Cox, *Military Reminiscences of the Civil War* (New York: Charles Scribner's Sons, 1900), p. 264.
2. Oliver O. Howard, *Autobiography of Oliver Otis Howard* (New York: The Baker & Taylor Company, 1907), p. 314.
3. Augustus Woodbury, *Major General Ambrose E. Burnside and the Ninth Army Corps* (Providence: Sidney S. Rider & Brother, 1867), pp. 3-173.
4. Thomas M. Spaulding, "Edwin Vose Sumner," *Dictionary of American Biography,* ed. Allen Johnson and Dumas Malone (New York: Charles Scribner's Sons, 1928-44), XVIII, pp. 214-15.
5. William A. Ganoe, "Joseph Hooker," *Dictionary of American Biography,* ed. Allen Johnson and Dumas Malone (New York: Charles Scribner's Sons, 1928-44), IX, pp. 196-97.
6. Thomas M. Spaulding, "William Buel Franklin," *Dictionary of American Biography,* ed. Allen Johnson and Dumas Malone (New York: Charles Scribner's Sons, 1928-44), VI, pp. 601-2.

7. Douglas S. Freeman, "Robert Edward Lee," *Dictionary of American Biography*, ed. Allen Johnson and Dumas Malone (New York: Charles Scribner's Sons, 1928-44), XI, pp. 120-24. See also Douglas S. Freeman, *R. E. Lee* (New York: Charles Scribner's Sons, 1935), Vols. I and II.

8. James Longstreet, *From Manassas to Appomattox* (2d ed.; Philadelphia: J. B. Lippincott Co., 1903), pp. 13-289.

9. Lt. Col. George F. R. Henderson, *Stonewall Jackson and the American Civil War* (New York: Longmans, Green, and Co., 1900), I, pp. 1-443 and II, pp. 1-285.

CHAPTER III

1. John C. Ropes, *The Story of the Civil War* (New York: G. P. Putnam's Sons, 1933), II, pp. 440-46.

2. Darius N. Couch, "Sumner's Right Grand Division," *Battles and Leaders of the Civil War*, ed. Robert U. Johnson and Clarence C. Buel (New York: The Century Co., 1888), III, p. 106.

3. Testimony of Maj. Gen. Ambrose E. Burnside, December 23, 1862, Report of the Joint Committee on the Conduct of the War, *Senate Reports*, No. 108 (Washington, D. C.: Government Printing Office, 1863), II, p. 650. Hereafter cited as Committee on the Conduct of the War.

4. Warren W. Hassler, Jr., *General George B. McClellan: Shield of the Union* (Baton Rouge: Louisiana State University Press, 1957), pp. 291-92.

5. Report of Maj. Gen. Burnside, Nov. 9, 1862, *O. R.*, p. 99.

6. *Ibid.*

7. Report of Maj. Gen. Halleck, November 15, 1863, *O. R.*, pp. 46-48.

8. Dispatch, Maj. Gen. Burnside to Maj. Gen. Halleck, December 17, 1862, *O. R.*, p. 67.

9. Report of Maj. Gen. Burnside, November 13, 1865, *O. R.*, p. 84.

10. Herman Haupt, *Reminiscences of General Herman Haupt* (Milwaukee: Wright and Joys Co., 1901), pp. 158-59.

11. Telegram, Maj. Gen. Halleck to Maj. Gen. Burnside, November 14, 1862, *O. R.*, p. 84.

12. Edward J. Stackpole, *Drama on the Rappahannock: The Fredericksburg Campaign* (Harrisburg, Pa.: The Military Service Publishing Co., 1957), p. 97. The order for removal of the pontoons from Berlin to Washington was sent by regular mail rather than by telegraph which caused the orders to be six days longer in arriving at the responsible engineer headquarters.

13. Dispatches, Maj. Gen. Burnside to Chief of Staff Cullum, November 19 and November 22, 1862, *O. R.*, pp. 101-4.

14. Letter, Maj. Gen. Hooker to Secretary of War Stanton, November 19, 1862, *O. R.*, pp. 773-74.

15. Report of Maj. Gen. Burnside, November 13, 1865, *O. R.*, p. 85.

16. Report of Gen. Lee, April 10, 1863, *O. R.*, p. 551.

17. Dispatch, Gen. Lee to Pres. Davis, November 25, 1862, *O. R.*, p. 1029.

18. Dispatch, Gen. Lee to Secretary of War Seddon, December 16, 1862, *O. R.*, p. 548.

19. Letter, Gen. Lee to Pres. Davis, November 25, 1862, *O. R.*, p. 1029.

CHAPTER IV

1. William Swinton, *Campaigns of the Army of the Potomac* (New York: Charles Scribner's Sons, 1882), pp. 235-38.

2. Dispatch, Lt. Cmdr. E. P. McCrea to Maj. Gen. John G. Parke, Chief of Staff, November 30, 1862, *O. R.*, p. 811.

3. Report of Maj. Gen. Burnside, November 13, 1865, *O. R.*, p. 87.

4. William F. Smith, "Franklin's Left Grand Division," *Battles and Leaders of the Civil War*, III, pp. 129-30.

5. Roy P .Basler (ed.), *The Collected Works of Abraham Lincoln* (New Brunswick, N. J.: Rutgers University Press, 1953), V, pp. 514-15.

6. G. F. R. Henderson, *The Campaign of Fredericksburg* (3d ed., London: Gale and Polden, Ltd. [1891]), p. 37.

7. Testimony of Maj. Gen. Edwin V. Sumner, December 19, 1862, Committee on the Conduct of the War, II, p. 658.

8. Report of Lt. Cyrus B. Comstock, December 20, 1862, *O. R.*, pp. 167-68.

9. Report of Maj. Gen. Burnside, November 13, 1865, *O. R.*, p. 88.

10. Report of Brig. Gen. Hunt, January 10, 1863, *O. R.*, pp. 180-81.

11. U. S. War Department, Board of Artillery Officers, *Instruction for Field Artillery* (Washington, D. C.: Government Printing Office, 1864), p. 36.

12. Report of Col. Tompkins, December 21, 1862, *O. R.*, p. 192, and Report of Col. Tyler, January 15, 1863, *O. R.*, p. 198.

13. Orders, Maj. Gen. Burnside to Maj. Gens. Franklin, Sumner, and Hooker, December 11, 1862, *O. R.*, p. 106.

14. Report of Maj. Gen. Burnside, November 13, 1865, *O. R.*, p. 88.

15. Report of Gen. Lee, April 10, 1863, *O. R.*, p. 551.

16. Oliver O. Howard, *Autobiography of Oliver Otis Howard* (New York: The Baker and Taylor Co., 1907), I, p. 321.

17. Frank Moore (ed.), *The Rebellion Record: A Diary of American Events* (New York: G. P. Putnam, 1863), VI, p. 95.

18. Randolph A. Shotwell, *The Papers of Randolph Abbott Shotwell* (Raleigh: The North Carolina Historical Commission, 1929), I, p. 393.

19. The term, "seeing the elephant," was frequently used during the Civil War to indicate initial exposure to combat. Recruits were often teased about how they would react to the experience.

CHAPTER V

1. E. Porter Alexander, *Military Memoirs of a Confederate* (New York: Charles Scribner's Sons, 1907), pp. 289-92.

2. Report of Lt. Charles E. Cross, December 18, 1862, *O. R.*, p. 169.

3. Report of Lt. Comstock, December 20, 1862, *O. R.*, pp. 167-68.

4. Lt. Col. E. Porter Alexander, "The Battle of Fredericksburg," *Papers, Southern Historical Society*, X (1882), p. 384.

5. Freeman, *Lee's Lieutenants*, II, pp. 332-38. See also *O. R.*, pp. 600-6.

6. William W. Blackford, *War Years with Jeb Stuart* (New York: Charles Scribner's Sons, 1945), p. 190.

7. Freeman, *Lee's Lieutenants*, II, pp. 333-34.

8. Report of Major Ira Spaulding, December 12, 1862, *O. R.*, p. 175.

9. Report of Brig. Gen. Hunt, January 10, 1863, *O. R.*, pp. 182-83.

10. Report of Maj. James A. Magruder, December 12, 1862, *O. R.*, pp. 173-74.

11. Report of Lt. Cross, December 18, 1862, *O. R.*, p. 169, and Report of Maj. Gen. Franklin, January 2, 1863, *O. R.*, pp. 448-49.

12. Report of Brig. Gen. Daniel P. Woodbury, December 12, 1862, *O. R.*, p. 169.

13. Report of Col. Tompkins, December 21, 1862, *O. R.*, p. 190.

14. Moore, *Rebellion Record*, VI, p. 248.

15. Major G. W. Redway, *Fredericksburg* (London: George Allen and Unwin, Ltd., 1906), pp. 99-100.

16. Report of Col. Tompkins, December 21, 1862, *O. R.*, p. 191.

17. Report of Brig. Gen. Hunt, January 10, 1863, *O. R.*, p. 183.

18. In the first assault wave there was a twelve-year-old drummer boy, Robert H. Henderson, who sneaked across by hanging onto one of the pontoon boats. He abandoned his drum for a musket once on land and captured a wounded Rebel. He was cheered by his comrades when he returned, escorting his prize to the Provost Marshal. Charles C. Coffin reports this incident in *Four Years of Fighting* (Boston: Ticknor and Fields, 1866), p. 149.

19. Report of Col. Norman J. Hall, December 17, 1862, *O. R.*, p. 282.

20. Report of Col. Hall, December 17, 1862, *O. R.*, p. 283.

21. Report of Col. Benjamin G. Humphreys, December 17, 1862, *O. R.*, p. 605.

22. H. G. O. Weymouth *et al.*, *History of the Nineteenth Regiment Massachusetts Volunteer Infantry* (Salem, Mass.: The Salem Press Co., 1906), p. 171, and George A. Bruce, *The Twentieth Regiment of Massachusetts Volunteer Infantry 1861-1865* (New York: Houghton Mifflin Company, 1906), pp. 1201-2. Among the first to fall in this charge was a citizen who had been pressed into service as a guide. Actually, he was one of the Rebel pickets who had been taken prisoner by the Seventh Michigan while he was sniping into the rear of the advance. Just at this moment, the Twentieth Massachusetts column of attack rushed by and the prisoner was carried along with it.

23. Report of Col. Hall, December 17, 1862, *O. R.*, p. 283.

24. Report of Col. Harrison S. Fairchild, December 17, 1862, *O. R.*, p. 345.

25. Robert Stiles, *Four Years Under Marse Robert* (New York: The Neale Publishing Company, 1903), p. 130.

26. Report of Brig. Gen. Devens, December 17, 1862, *O. R.*, p. 536.

27. Report of Brig. Gen. Howard, December 19, 1862, *O. R.*, p. 262.

28. Report of Lt. Comstock, December 20, 1862, *O. R.*, p. 168.

29. Report of Lt. Col. Edgar A. Kimball, December 16, 1862, *O. R.*, p. 344.

30. Joseph R. Ward, *History of the 106th Regiment Pennsylvania Volunteers* (Philadelphia: F. McManus, Jr. and Co., 1906), pp. 133-35.

31. *Ibid.*, pp. 132-33.

32. Report of Lt. Gen. Longstreet, December 20, 1862, *O. R.*, p. 571.

33. On December 12, 1862, daylight began about 6 a.m., *O. R.*, p. 485.

34. Report of Maj. Gen. Franklin, January 2, 1863, *O. R.*, p. 449.

35. Report of Brig. Gen. Hunt, January 10, 1863, *O. R.*, p. 184.

36. Report of Maj. Gen. Sumner, January 14, 1863, *O. R.*, p. 219.

37. Report of Brig. Gen. Hunt, January 10, 1863, *O. R.*, p. 184.

38. Report of Lt. Gen. Jackson, January 31, 1863, *O. R.*, p. 630.

CHAPTER VI

1. This road was also identified on contemporary maps as the Old Richmond Stage Road, the Bowling Green Road, and the River Road.
2. This road was also known as the Orange Turnpike or simply the Plank Road.
3. U. S. Army Map Service, 1:25,000, Guinea Sheet 5560 III NW (Washington, D. C.: 1949); and U. S. Army Map Service, 1:25,000, Fredericksburg Sheet IV SW (Washington, D. C.: 1946). See also *Atlas to Accompany the Official Records of the Union and Confederate Armies* (Washington, D. C.: Government Printing Office, 1891-1895), Plate XXXIII, No. 1; and Report of Brig. Gen. Hunt, January 10, 1863, *O. R.*, pp. 180-81.

CHAPTER VII

1. Report of Maj. Gen. Burnside, November 13, 1865, *O. R.*, p. 89.
2. Testimony of Maj. Gen. Franklin, December 19, 1862, Committee on the Conduct of the War, II, p. 707.
3. Report of Maj. Gen. Burnside, November 13, 1865, *O. R.*, p. 90.
4. Jubal A. Early, *Autobiographical Sketch and Narrative of the War Between the States* (Philadelphia: J. B. Lippincott Co., 1912), p. 183.
5. One additional possibility existed for General Burnside in this situation. He could have shifted Hooker's Grand Division upriver to make a crossing by the fords north of Falmouth in an attempt to maneuver Lee out of position. This would have required engineer support and additional bridging which could be made available only at the cost of additional delay. It would also have left the main body open to attack by Lee while the flanking movement was in progress.
6. R. Ernest Dupuy and Trevor N. Dupuy, *Military Heritage of America* (New York: McGraw-Hill Book Co., Inc., 1956), p. 258.
7. Moore, *Rebellion Record*, VI, p. 98.
8. Some students of the battle indicate, in addition to this marshy area, the presence of a large ice pond just west of the canal ditch between William and Hanover Streets. This ice pond shows on some maps of Fredericksburg made after 1870. However, a careful check of the property deeds on file in the City Court House failed to corroborate the presence of the pond as early as 1862.
9. Report of Maj. Gen. Burnside, November 13, 1865, *O. R.*, pp. 90-91.
10. Testimony of Maj. Gen. Burnside, Committee on the Conduct of the War, December 23, 1862, II, p. 652.
11. The word "seize" in Franklin's order indicates that Burnside felt that Prospect Hill was only lightly held, since the word "carry" was used in ordering troops to attack strongly-held positions. This possibly indicates that Burnside still thought Lee's army was divided and extended downriver to Port Royal.
12. Report of Maj. Gen. Burnside, November 13, 1865, *O. R.*, pp. 90-91.
13. Letter from Capt. Frederick Beardslee to his father, G. W. Beardslee, *Beardslee's Military Telegraph* (New York: John A. Gray and Green, 1863), pp. 13-14. This pamphlet was compiled and issued by the Beardslee Magneto-Electric Company.

14. Report of Thaddeus S. C. Lowe, May 26, 1863, *O. R.*, (1902), Series III, Vol. III, p. 294. This reference is an exception to the procedure outlined in footnote 2, for p. 1.

15. U. S. Surgeon-General's Office, *The Medical and Surgical History of the War of the Rebellion* (Second Issue, Washington, D. C.: Government Printing Office, 1875), Appendix, Part I, pp. 102-34.

16. Report of Brig Gen. Rufus Ingalls, Chief Quartermaster, Army of the Potomac, March 19, 1864, *O. R.*, pp. 147-48.

CHAPTER VIII

1. Report of Lt. Gen. Jackson, January 31, 1863, *O. R.*, pp. 630-31.

2. Major John W. McDonald, Cavalry, U. S. Army, "The Battle of Fredericksburg" (unpublished manuscript, Fredericksburg and Spotsylvania National Military Park Museum, Fredericksburg, Va., n.d.), p. 9.

3. Alexander, *Papers, Southern Historical Society,* X, p. 384.

4. Abstract from field return of the Department of Northern Virginia, December 10, 1862, *O. R.*, p. 1057.

5. Report of Maj. Gen. Reynolds, December 21, 1862, *O. R.*, pp. 452-54.

6. Report of Maj. Gen. Meade, December 20, 1862, *O. R.*, pp. 510-11.

7. Heros Von Borcke, *Memoirs of the Confederate War for Independence* (New York: Peter Smith, 1938), pp. 117-19.

8. Report of Brig. Gen. Doubleday, December 22, 1862, *O. R.*, pp. 461-62.

9. Report of Maj. Gen. Daniel H. Hill, December 24, 1862, *O. R.*, p. 643.

10. Report of Maj. Gen. John Gibbon, March 7, 1863, *O. R.*, p. 480.

11. Von Borcke, *Memoirs,* p. 117.

12. The brigade line of battle consisted of each regiment of the brigade in a single line, with each regiment in a formation two lines deep. The brigade in this formation would appear to be two long lines of soldiers, the long axis of the line facing the enemy.

13. Report of Maj. Gen. Reynolds, December 21, 1862, *O. R.*, pp. 453-54.

14. Freeman, *Lee's Lieutenants,* II, pp. 351-52.

15. Report of Maj. Gen. Franklin, January 2, 1863, *O. R.*, p. 450.

16. Abner R. Small, *The Road to Richmond* (Berkeley: University of California Press, 1939), p. 65.

17. Report of Brig. Gen. Birney, December 17, 1862, *O. R.*, pp. 361-62.

18. Report of Maj. Gen. Meade, December 20, 1862, *O. R.*, pp. 509-13; and Report of Lt. Gen. Jackson, January 31, 1863, *O. R.*, p. 632.

19. Report of Brig. Gen. Gibbon, March 7, 1863, *O. R.*, p. 480.

20. Report of Col. Root, December 23, 1862, *O. R.*, pp. 485-87.

21. Report of Maj. Gen. Franklin, January 2, 1863, *O. R.*, p. 450.

22. Report of Lt. Gen. Jackson, January 31, 1863, *O. R.*, pp. 632-33.

23. Report of Brig. Gen. Birney, December 17, 1862, *O. R.*, pp. 361-63.

24. Report of Maj. Gen. Franklin, January 2, 1863, *O. R.*, pp. 450-51.

25. Statement of Capt. R. H. I. Goddard, April 3, 1863, *O. R.*, p. 128.

26. Report of Maj. Gen. Burnside, November 13, 1865, *O. R.*, p. 118.

27. Report of Maj. Gen. Franklin, January 2, 1863, *O. R.*, pp. 450-51.

28. Report of Maj. Gen. Reynolds, December 21, 1862, *O. R.*, p. 455.
29. Early, *Autobiographical Sketch*, p. 178.
30. Von Borcke, *Memoirs*, p. 129.
31. Smith, *Battles and Leaders*, III, pp. 135-37.
32. Return of casualties in the Union forces, *O. R.*, pp. 135-37.
33. Report of Lt. M. R. Baldwin, December 27, 1862, *O. R.*, p. 1122.

CHAPTER IX

1. William Boston, *Civil War Diary of William Boston* (Ann Arbor, Michigan: Orlan Boston, 1937), p. 14.
2. Couch, *Battles and Leaders*, III, pp. 108-9.
3. Report of Lt. Gen. Longstreet, December 20, 1862, *O. R.*, pp. 568-69.
4. Report of Col. Walton, December 30, 1862, *O. R.*, pp. 573-74.
5. Haupt, *Reminiscences*, pp. 182-83.
6. Map of Fredericksburg, *The National Atlas* (Philadelphia: O. W. Gray and Son, 1878), p. 374; and Report of Gen. Lee, April 10, 1863, *O. R.*, pp. 552-53.
7. James Longstreet, "The Battle of Fredericksburg," *Battles and Leaders*, III, p. 79.
8. Report of Maj. Gen. Couch, January, 1863, *O. R.*, pp. 222-23; and Report of Col. John S. Mason, December 17, 1862, *O. R.*, p. 291.
9. Report of Lt. Col. James Huston, December 17, 1862, *O. R.*, p. 291.
10. Howard, *Autobiography*, p. 338.
11. Franklin probably had not sent any reports since his attack was not really underway at this time. General Hardie, Burnside's staff representative, apparently saw no need for reporting either, although later in the day he made prolific use of the telegraph to inform his chief of the situation on Franklin's front.
12. Statement of Capt. P. M. Lydig, March 31, 1863, *O. R.*, p. 127.
13. Report of Maj. Gen. Burnside, November 13, 1865, *O. R.*, p. 94.
14. Report of Brig. Gen. French, December 18, 1862, *O. R.*, p. 287.
15. Report of Capt. Diedrichs, December 19, 1862, *O. R.*, p. 201.
16. Report of Brig. Gen. Winfield S. Hancock, December 25, 1862, *O. R.*, pp. 226-27.
17. Report of Col. Mason, December 17, 1862, *O. R.*, p. 291.
18. Report of Brig. Gen. Kimball, December 22, 1862, *O. R.*, p. 290.
19. Report of Col. Marshall, December 18, 1862, *O. R.*, p. 305.
20. There was not sufficient space behind the protecting bluff west of the canal ditch to deploy more than one brigade at a time and still maintain the integrity of the line of battle.
21. Report of Col. Palmer, December 18, 1862, *O. R.*, p. 300.
22. Couch, *Battles and Leaders*, III, p. 113.
23. Report of Brig. Gen. Hunt, January 10, 1863, *O. R.*, p. 184.
24. Report of Col. Zook, December 20, 1862, *O. R.*, pp. 253-54.
25. Longstreet, *Battles and Leaders*, III, p. 81.

26. Lafayette McLaws, "The Confederate Left at Fredericksburg," *Battles and Leaders*, III, pp. 91-93.

27. Report of Brig. Gen. Meagher, December 20, 1862, *O. R.*, p. 240.

28. Report of Brig. Gen. Caldwell, January 21, 1863, *O. R.*, pp. 232-33.

29. Report of Col. Edward E. Cross, December 15, 1862, *O. R.*, p. 235.

30. Report of Lt. Col. David B. McCreary, December 20, 1862, *O. R.*, p. 239.

31. Report of Brig. Gen. Hancock, December 25, 1862, *O. R.*, p. 227.

32. Report of Maj. Gen. Couch, January, 1863, *O. R.*, p. 221.

33. Report of Col. Owen, December 18, 1862, *O. R.*, pp. 278-79.

34. Report of Col. Hall, December 17, 1862, *O. R.*, p. 282.

35. *Ibid.*, p. 284.

36. Report of Brig. Gen. Howard, December 19, 1862, *O. R.*, p. 263.

37. Couch, *Battles and Leaders*, III, p. 113.

38. Report of Lt. Gen. Longstreet, December 20, 1862, *O. R.*, p. 570.

39. Report of Maj. Gen. McLaws, December 30, 1862, *O. R.*, p. 579.

40. Report of Brig. Gen. Willcox, January 7, 1863, *O. R.*, pp. 311-12.

41. Leander W. Cogswell, *A History of the Eleventh New Hampshire Regiment Volunteer Infantry in the Rebellion War* (Concord, N. H.: Republican Press Association, 1891), p. 54.

42. Thomas H. Parker, *History of the 51st Regiment of P. V. and V. V.* (Philadelphia: King and Baird, 1869), p. 280.

43. Report of Brig. Gen. Ferrero, December 16, 1862, *O. R.*, pp. 325-26.

44. Report of Brig. Gen. Sturgis, December 24, 1862, *O. R.*, pp. 316-17.

45. Report of Brig. Gen. Nagle, December 16, 1862, *O. R.*, pp. 319-20.

46. Report of Brig. Gen. Willcox, January 7, 1863, *O. R.*, p. 312.

47. Report of Brig. Gen. Whipple, December 18, 1862, *O. R.*, p. 393.

48. Report of Maj. Gen. Hooker, September 5, 1863, *O. R.*, p. 356.

49. Testimony of Maj. Gen. Hooker, December 20, 1862, Committee on the Conduct of the War, II, p. 668.

50. Haupt, *Reminiscences*, p. 183.

51. Report of Brig. Gen. Hunt, January 10, 1863, *O. R.*, p. 185.

52. Report of Maj. Gen. Hooker, September 5, 1863, *O. R.*, pp. 356-57.

53. Report of Brig. Gen. Griffin, December 16, 1862, *O. R.*, pp. 404-5.

54. Wise, *The Long Arm of Lee*, I, p. 396.

55. Report of Col. Allabach, December 19, 1862, *O. R.*, pp. 443-44. Allabach indicated in this report that his men advanced to within twelve yards of the stone wall; but, based on Confederate and Union reports, it is the writer's estimate that these troops did not actually get closer than fifty yards.

56. Report of Brig. Gen. Humphreys, December 16, 1862, *O. R.*, pp. 431-32.

57. David W. Rowe, *A Sketch of the 126th Regiment Pennsylvania Volunteers* (Chambersburg, Pa.: Cook and Hays, 1869), p. 18.

58. Report of Brig. Gen. Tyler, December 16, 1862, *O. R.*, p. 437.

59. Ward, *History of the 106th Regiment*, p. 142.

60. Report of Brig. Gen. Sykes, December 20, 1862, *O. R.*, p. 415.

61. Alexander, *Papers, Southern Historical Society*, X, p. 456.

62. Report of Brig. Gen. Ransom, December 20, 1862, *O. R.*, p. 626.

63. Report of Col. Hawkins, December 19, 1862, *O. R.*, p. 336.

64. Report of Col. Harland, December 17, 1862, *O. R.*, p. 348.

65. Moore, *Rebellion Record*, VI, p. 50.
66. Order from Brig. Gen. Butterfield to Brig. Gen. Sykes, December 13, 1862, *O. R.*, p. 117.
67. Henry Steele Commager (ed), *The Blue and the Gray* (Indianapolis, Ind.: The Bobbs-Merrill Company, Inc., 1950), I, p. 247.
68. Ward, *History of the 106th Regiment*, p. 146.
69. Frederick L. Hitchcock, *War from the Inside* (Philadelphia: J. B. Lippincott Company, 1904), p. 127.
70. Stiles, *Four Years Under Marse Robert*, p. 137.
71. Testimony of Maj. Gen. Burnside, December 19, 1862, Committee on the Conduct of the War, II, p. 653.

CHAPTER X

1. Testimony of Maj. Gen. Burnside, December 19, 1862, Committee on the Conduct of the War, II, p. 653.
2. William Todd, *The Seventy-Ninth Highlanders New York Volunteers in the War of the Rebellion* (Albany: Press of Brandoro, Barton and Co., 1886), p. 264.
3. Couch, *Battles and Leaders*, III, p. 117.
4. Telegram, Maj. Gen. Burnside to Pres. Lincoln, December 14, 1862, *O. R.*, p. 65.
5. Testimony of Maj. Gen. Burnside, December 19, 1862, Committee on the Conduct of the War, II, p. 653.
6. *Ibid.*
7. Alexander, *Military Memoirs*, p. 311.
8. John W. Ames, "In Front of the Stone Wall," *Battles and Leaders*, III, pp. 122-23.
9. Report of Capt. Hiram Dryer, December 19, 1862, *O. R.*, pp. 421-22.
10. Report of Lt. Col. Robert C. Buchanan, December 19, 1862, *O. R.*, pp. 418-19.
11. Survivors Association, 118th Pennsylvania, *Antietam to Appomattox* (Philadelphia: J. L. Smith, 1892), pp. 132-34.
12. Report of Capt. John D. Wilkins, December 19, 1862, *O. R.*, p. 420.
13. D. P. Conyngham, *The Irish Brigade and Its Campaigns* (New York: William McSorley and Co., 1867), pp. 330 and 332.
14. William E. Barton, *The Life of Clara Barton* (New York: Houghton Mifflin Co., 1922), I, p. 218.
15. Report of Col. George H. Sharpe, December 17, 1862, *O. R.*, p. 388.
16. Telegram, Brig. Gen. Hardie to Maj. Gen. Burnside, December 14, 1862, *O. R.*, p. 120.
17. Report of Brig. Gen. Sickles, December 18, 1862, *O. R.*, p. 381.
18. Dispatch, Gen. Lee to Secretary Seddon, December 13, 1862, *O. R.*, p. 546.
19. Report of Lt. Gen. Longstreet, December 20, 1862, *O. R.*, p. 571.
20. Report of Lt. Gen. Jackson, January 31, 1863, *O. R.*, p. 634.
21. William W. Blackford, *War Years with Jeb Stuart* (New York: Charles Scribner's Sons, 1945), p. 196.
22. Edward S. Ellis, *The Campfires of General Lee* (Philadelphia: Henry Harrison and Company, 1886), pp. 222-24.

23. Order, Maj. Gen. Hooker to Brig. Gen. Averell, December 10, 1862, *O. R.*, p. 845.

24. Report of Brig. Gen. Pleasonton, January 12, 1863, *O. R.*, pp. 220-21.

25. Return of the Army of the Potomac for December 10, 1862, *O. R.*, p. 1121.

26. Correspondence between Maj. Gen. Burnside and Maj. Gen Sigel, *O. R.*, pp. 847-50. The troops of both these corps were acting as advance elements of the Washington garrison, although they were under Burnside's control. He made no attempt to bring them closer until too late for them to arrive in time to be of value. Burnside gave no indication that he felt their presence would have been of value to him, seemingly a very strange attitude for a commanding general. His orders to Sigel and Slocum on December 13 seem more like the afterthought of a general who had suddenly remembered the presence of a 33,000-man reserve.

27. Couch, *Battles and Leaders*, III, pp. 117-18.

28. Gideon Welles, *Diary* (Boston: Houghton Mifflin Co., 1911), I, pp. 191-92.

29. Louis M. Starr, *Bohemian Brigade* (New York: Alfred A. Knopf, 1954), p. 167.

30. Haupt, *Reminiscences*, p. 177.

31. Dispatch from Gen. Halleck to Maj. Gen. Burnside, December 15, 1862, *O. R.*, p. 122.

32. Order from Maj. Gen. Burnside to Brig. Gen. Couch, December 14, 1862, *O. R.*, p. 121.

33. Alexander, *Military Memoirs*, p. 312.

34. Warren H. Cudworth, *History of the First Regiment Massachusetts Infantry* (Boston: Walker, Fuller and Co., 1866), p. 323.

35. Circular from Headquarters of Maj. Gen. Hooker, December 15, 1862, *O. R.*, p. 123.

36. Survivors Association, *Antietam to Appomattox*, p. 137.

37. Todd, *Seventy-Ninth Highlanders*, p. 265.

38. Charles H. Weygant, *History of the One Hundred and Twenty-Fourth Regiment NYSV* (Newburgh, N. Y.: Journal Printing House, 1877), p. 68.

39. Report of Maj. Gen. Franklin, January 2, 1863, *O. R.*, p. 451.

40. Report of Brig. Gen. Butterfield, December, 1862, *O. R.*, p. 401.

41. Cudworth, *History of the First Massachusetts*, pp. 325-26.

42. William A. Fletcher, *Rebel Private Front and Rear* (Austin, Texas: University of Texas Press, 1954), p. 51.

43. Report of Brig. Gen. Butterfield, December, 1862, *O. R.*, p. 401.

44. Von Borcke, *Memoirs*, p. 143.

45. Robert E. Lee, *Recollections and Letters of General Robert E. Lee* (New York: Doubleday, Page and Co., 1909), pp. 86-87. In the last sentence of Lee's letter, the word "it" apparently refers to the completeness of the victory Lee had won.

46. G. Moxley Sorrel, *Recollections of a Confederate Staff Officer* (2d ed., New York: The Neale Publishing Company, 1917), pp. 144-45.

47. Livermore, *Numbers and Losses*, p. 96. A detailed breakdown of the casualties for both armies will be found in Appendix B.

48. Report of Maj. Gen. Burnside, December 17, 1862, *O. R.*, p. 67.

49. Message from President Lincoln to the Army of the Potomac, December 22, 1862, *O. R.*, pp. 67-68.

APPENDIX A

1. Organization of the Union Forces, *O. R.*, pp. 48-61.
2. Organization of Confederate Forces, *O. R.*, pp. 538-45.

APPENDIX B

1. Return of casualties for Battle of Fredericksburg, *O. R.*, pp. 129-42.
2. Report of Medical Director, Army of Northern Virginia, January 10, 1863, *O. R.*, pp. 558-62.
3. Table of Losses, Confederate Army, *Battles and Leaders*, III, pp. 146-47. Figures for this column only were taken from this source since numbers of missing were not included in *O. R.*, report.

APPENDIX C

1. Report of Maj. Gen. Hooker, September 5, 1863, *O. R.*, p. 357.
2. A movement on multiple axes means that a military force is moving in separate detachments toward a common objective but over several different roads.
3. Testimony of Maj. Gen. Franklin, Committee on the Conduct of the War, December 19, 1862, II, p. 662.
4. Letter from Gen. Lee to Pres. Davis, November 25, 1862, *O. R.*, p. 1029.
5. None of the grand division commanders had received positive information concerning the enemy positions. In the absence of these facts, Sumner and Franklin were ready to execute Burnside's plans without question. General Hooker was convinced that crossing the river would bring disaster, but as a soldier he was ready to obey orders.
6. Report of Lt. Comstock, December 20, 1862, *O. R.*, pp. 167-68.
7. Couch, *Battles and Leaders*, III, p. 308.
8. Testimony of Maj. Gen. Franklin, December 19, 1862, Committee on the Conduct of the War, II, p. 707.
9. Barron Deaderick, *Strategy in the Civil War* (Harrisburg, Pa.: The Military Service Publishing Company, 1951), p. 61.
10. Among the commentators accepting this view are G. F. R. Henderson, Trevor N. Dupuy, T. Harry Williams, and John C. Ropes.
11. Dispatch from Brig. Gen. Ingalls to Brig. Gen. Meigs, December 16, 1862, *O. R.*, p. 858.
12. Stuart's cavalry forces suffered only thirteen casualties during the whole operation (Casualty return, Confederate army, *O. R.*, p. 562), yet they were so active that they constantly threatened the safety of Doubleday's line.
13. Longstreet, *From Manassas to Appomattox*, p. 315.
14. Testimony of Maj. Gen. Meade, Committee on the Conduct of the War, March 16, 1863, II, p. 691.
15. Starr, *Bohemian Brigade*, p. 164.
16. Testimony of Maj. Gen. Hooker, Committee on the Conduct of the War, December 20, 1862, II, p. 669.
17. Parker, *History of the 51st Regiment of P. V. and V. V.*, p. 280.